CAREER *Clarity*

FINALLY FIND THE WORK THAT FITS YOUR VALUES & LIFESTYLE

LISA LEWIS MILLER

Career Clarity LLC, P.O. Box 1312 Westminster, CO 80036-1312

First hardcover edition November 2020
Book design by Laura Murray Creative

ISBN 978-1-7355861-1-3 (paperback)
ISBN 978-1-7355861-0-6 (hardcover)
ISBN 978-1-7355861-3-7 (audiobook)
ISBN 978-1-7355861-2-0 (EPUB eBook)

www.GetCareerClarity.com

Advanced Praise:

"Lisa Miller's Career Clarity framework is life-changing. If you're someone who has struggled to find a career that feels like home, this book is for you. Lisa not only gives you a roadmap to combine your personality, interests, strengths, and skills into a profitable career that lights you up, but also fortifies your confidence and mindset along the way."

- Melody Wilding, MSW, TEDx speaker and author of *Trust Yourself*

"Life is both too short and too long to not love your work. Lisa gets this in a deep and powerful way. Best of all, she's written a book that isn't theoretical platitudes but a practical roadmap for how you can actually (finally) do the most meaningful work of your life. If you're underfulfilled with your work in any way, get this book and devour it immediately."

- Josh Allan Dykstra, CEO of Helios

"Does work feel a bit (or a lot!) off? Are you looking for the optimal career fit for every piece of you, including your lifestyle? Sought-after career coach Lisa Miller has created the premier system to get you there, filled with realistic, compelling, attainable steps. In her first book, Lisa hasn't just innovated — she's completely shattered the career search mold."

- Rebecca Fraser-Thill, senior contributor at *Forbes Careers* and psychology instructor at Bates College

"Lisa Lewis Miller's book, *Career Clarity*, guides the reader through a proven three-step process to career SANITY. She teaches that it's not about finding ONE dream job but enabling confident clarity about your values and finding a values match. Her process enables experimentation, piloting yourself through better and better career matches over time to arrive at a deeply satisfying career."

- S. Chris Edmonds, speaker, author, and consultant

"As an HR nerd, this book had me nodding my head so many times. If you just got a new job and have realized the grass isn't greener or keep feeling a calling to do something different, this book will help you figure out what and why. We spend so much time at work and yet we rarely take the time to do the research and preparation required. Lisa talks us through her 4 Pillars framework of not only why this is important but how it will make you happier in the long run."

- Janice Chaka, CEO of Introvert Media Lab

"If you know deep down that you're unhappy in your work, this book will do more than just inspire you to take action — it will show you the path to a better, more satisfying career. With a warm heart and practical suggestions, *Career Clarity* will demystify the process of discovering a career you can be truly passionate about."

- Dr. Nick Wignall, clinical psychologist and author

"The worst part about going through a career crisis is believing that you're alone in the process. Lisa's willingness to be vulnerable about her own story and her clients' experiences shines a light on how common these moments really are. I needed this book as an academic overachiever who thought I was supposed to have it all together. This book has the perfect scaffolding to help you get up and take the next best, practical steps."

- Caitlin Faas, PhD

"Before you work on your resume, STOP! Read this book first. Using 4 Pillars of Career Fulfillment, *Career Clarity* invites job seekers to get clear on their next move — and embark on the 'professional road less traveled.' This is the book I wish I had before applying for any job or even starting my own business! Fueled by powerful stories and examples, Lisa Miller encourages the reader to be courageous (and even a little rebellious) so they can get what they want from their career."

- Chris Villanueva, CEO of Let's Eat, Grandma

"This book is packed with relatable examples of a proven framework that can be used over and over again throughout your career. It's a must-read for anyone ready to fill their days with meaningful work!"

- Jenn Smith, HR expert and CEO of Flourish Careers

"If you're seeking career fulfillment, you've come to the right place. Let Lisa Lewis Miller guide the way with a playbook to help you find work you love that pays the bills."

- Adam Smiley Poswolsky, author of *The Quarter-Life Breakthrough*

"*Career Clarity* by Lisa Lewis Miller is a straight-forward, accessible, approachable solution for anyone who wants more clarity and less confusion in their career. Lisa is a gift to our industry and her work changes lives. Don't suffer alone. Reading *Career Clarity* will help you feel like you have the friend you need to help you succeed."

- Tracy Timm, author of *Unstoppable* and founder of The Nth Degree® Career Academy

"This isn't just a book about the next step in your career. This is an insightful framework that will lead toward fulfillment in your career and life for years. Buy it. Read it. Do it. You'll be thankful you did."

- Scott Anthony Barlow, CEO and founder, Happen To Your Career

Table Of Contents

Foreword

If change is the only constant, let's get better at it.

This is our new imperative when it comes to making career shifts, especially as technological innovation and globalization continue to change the world at such a rapid clip. The bad news: career certainty and stability have always been a myth. Upheaval is accelerating, resulting in increasingly frequent changes that can feel confusing and anxiety-provoking, and anything can happen at any time. The good news: we are all strengthening our skills to navigate the underlying reality of careers during the best or worst of times. By picking up this book, you're taking a wise step to prepare yourself to proactively pivot in ways large and small as you plan your career, creative projects, and next moves.

When the pandemic hit in 2020, it shook the world in unprecedented ways. Nobody was exempt: we all got pivoted. Maybe you were a twenty-something who graduated virtually, a frontline essential worker navigating terrifying health concerns, an employee working remotely (some while simultaneously juggling care for small children), or a small business owner like me who lost 75% of a typical year's revenue. Within a few months we all came to a shocking realization: there was no more "normal" to return to, not even a "new normal" to stand on. The "normal" ship had sailed once and for all, along with any answers about what the future might hold.

As you'll read in the pages ahead, even when you do land a "perfect on paper" opportunity, you might grow out of it due to your success. Imagine that! For some, success (however defined) can be harder to grapple with than the hurdles it took to get there. No one is exempt from the existential searching that career changes tend to inspire, and with good reason: work is where we spend the most time and energy. To add to the pressure, our ability to provide for ourselves can make career change feel like a quest for survival, a matter of life and death. But it doesn't have to. You can get better at pivoting, navigating this process, accelerating how you reach career clarity.

As Lisa writes in the introduction, some of the people who look shiniest and happiest are furiously paddling beneath the water, chasing after the hungry ghosts of adoration, admiration, and approval. As the saying goes, "Don't compare your full-length movie to someone else's highlight reel." Your path towards a fulfilling career is yours alone, but a book like this can certainly help you pave the way, with many time- and sanity-saving tips throughout. After knowing Lisa for nearly a decade, I have watched her voraciously learn, grow, apply, stretch, and share her wisdom at so many of the exciting stages along her career journey—from pivoting internally by creating a new coaching role for herself, to building a side hustle while mentoring with other coaches, to launching her own thriving practice, and now to sharing her wisdom with all of you through this book and her podcast.

Lisa cares deeply about your fulfillment and about helping clear the messy path of research and realizations so you can land something you love even faster. A self-described learning junkie, she has synthesized years of seeking into a three-part journey that starts *now*. There is no better time. We are all in the same boat as we create a new future together, given that the "normal" ship has sailed. Lisa is living proof that career clarity starts exactly as you are: with curiosity, a willingness to grapple with big meaty questions without fearing the answers, and with a belief that what you want to create *is* possible. I know I speak for both of us when I say: we can't wait to see where you take things from here!

To your next moves,

Jenny Blake, author of *Pivot: The Only Move That Matters Is Your Next One*, September 2020

Introduction

We all want to tell a beautiful — and honest — story about our career choices. We want to be able to gush with authentic excitement over what we do, and why.

Some people have a talent for making everything sound gushy and picture perfect: constantly "humble bragging" about winning awards, traveling to cool locations for business meetings, or working with enviable clients. They're the people who land on the "30 under 30" or "40 under 40" lists and share memes like: "Love your job and you'll never work a day in your life!"

Depending on what you say and how you say it, you can easily paint your career like it's a fairytale Disney movie, even if it's not.

10 years ago, I could have spun a similar, seemingly impressive tale about my professional trajectory. In the course of two and a half years, I went from a nonprofit job with little growth potential to doubling my salary by becoming a communications consultant. I traveled to Canada, England, and Indonesia, teaching businesses how to create advocacy campaigns and mobilize the public in favor of policy change.

Sounds pretty exciting, right? It hit the trifecta of covetable careers: great pay, tons of accolades, and ritzy international travel opportunities.

But there's a catch. (There's almost always a catch.)

Our words have power — especially the words we don't say. And that shiny Hollywood story above is the product of some serious lies of omission.

When I'm more honest about the pivot I'd made in my career, the lies of omission become much clearer: while I was on track to be a vice president by 28, I kept feeling like something was missing. As a communications consultant working down the street from the White House, I was basically a mercenary and hired gun tasked to spin media gaffes or public policy issues so they appeared to be in my clients' political favor. My job required me to work on whatever problem came through our doors, whether or not I agreed with the goals or beliefs. I felt like I was freely trading my own principles for a fast-tracked, externally impressive corporate career, and as long as I was comfortable with selling out, I could keep rocketing up the corporate ladder.

In short: I was unhappy, unfulfilled, and constantly questioning whether my work had any real value. Nobody else could see how conflicted I was about being great at work that tore me up inside.

Through this lens, it's clear the story is certainly not the same fairytale anymore. What it lacks in a cartoon heroine, it makes up for in honesty.

For many of us, our current career story doesn't sound so rosy. We don't want to stay on the same path for the rest of our days, and it can feel like the only way to have a career we love is by pretending and seriously filtering how we talk about our lives. We know those forced, airbrushed stories aren't real and aren't sustainable for the remaining decades of our careers, but don't know what else to do.

And yet, we know there are people out there who have taken courageous actions to create genuinely wonderful — and honest — new career stories.

People like Ron, an engineer in Portland who felt like his career and life in Oregon was starting to stall out when his wife suddenly landed a coveted tenured academic position in Seattle. To top things off, they found out they were expecting their first child. Ron's current job wasn't going to let him work remotely, and certainly didn't have an impressive paternity leave policy. Ron was staring down a career crossroads: he wanted to support his wife's career and relocate to Seattle where a lot of his family lived, but he didn't have any prospects in the area. He knew spending precious time with his first child was non-negotiable, and he wanted to make a change to make more money, but wasn't sure where to start. He used this framework to get clear on his priorities and options to better align his career with his life, and then took serious action: researching future prospective employers in Seattle remotely, repositioning himself as a leader and project manager, and negotiating his first six-figure job offer as well as six full weeks of bonus paternity leave.

Deja is another great example. Today, ex-pat Deja is based in London and is in charge of giving away millions of dollars to charities doing corporate social responsibility for an international media company. But her career started on a very different trajectory: doing events and management work for musicians in the United States. By doubling down on creating a courageous vision for the work and impact she wanted, and following the steps you'll learn in Phase 3 of this book to perfection, she paired her clear career direction with an all-out networking campaign that opened incredible doors for her to lead and grow abroad. (You'll meet oodles of other clients in the pages to follow. While the stories and details are authentic, their names are changed.)

Neither Ron nor Deja need a filter to make their careers and lives look amazing anymore. They were willing to take unconventional steps to define success on their own terms, create career paths that fit, and put in the work to make it happen. And they're thrilled with how things turned out!

I want that for you, too. Because if you're reading this book, you probably aren't completely in love with your job.

You've probably been a pretty good worker (maybe even labeled as an overachiever). Your career might look pretty impressive or jealousy-worthy on the outside.

But if we get really honest, that career doesn't feel as amazing on the inside.

It isn't that you completely hate your work, but you want a challenge you aren't getting. You feel like you aren't living up to your full potential. You're antsy for a change. And while you're not used to feeling this persistent itch of discontent, you're really starting to pay attention to it now.

Let me be the first to tell you: nothing is wrong with you. Breathe.

Your feelings are right — this role doesn't fit you.

Maybe you outgrew it, or maybe it never fit quite right to begin with.

So if you've been measuring yourself against Dylan, the sweet and determined young sprout who knew at the tender age of seven that he wanted to be a dentist, you can stop. Choosing to go to grad school and have a 40-year career in dentistry until you throw a retirement party in your 60s might work for some of your peers, but it's not the right path for you. And that's okay.

In fact, that might even be good: wanting to keep growing, stretching, and learning new things is good for you, good for your work, and good for our economy. Your desire to learn is one of the key drivers of the Career Clarity approach to career pathing. This book wouldn't have caught your eye if you didn't want to learn how to make a change.

You can trust your feeling that you want work to feel better. You *aren't* meant to settle. You don't want to become one of those people with the dead look in their eyes, for whom every day at work is "same shit, different day" — or worse: "fine."

I've been in your shoes. As an obsessive learner and overachiever, I would devour books, podcasts, TED Talks, and online courses to try to understand the secret keys to creating a fulfilling, juicy, life-giving career path, because my work felt so life-draining.

There are a lot of books out there. Some writers focus on the tactical pieces, like getting job offers or professional rebranding. Others teach you how to follow your heart. But while most thought leaders presented their strategies to solve a particular issue along the career journey, I noticed few people were effectively looking at the start-to-finish journey. As much as they entertain or encourage, they often don't zoom out enough to give you the full picture of why you haven't found fulfilling work you love — and how to land that fantastic job without going broke.

After collecting the data points from other experts, I went on to use that research to help more than 500 clients make successful career transitions of their own. This experience taught me a lot about what actually works (and doesn't) for finding lucrative, soulful, and joyful work. With the lessons learned from seeing hundreds of individuals on this professional pilgrimage, I synthesized the full body of work into the Career Clarity methodology. This book shares that strategic framework with you, so you can master how to find great work and create a satisfying, delightful career that empowers you to live your best life, step by step.

The Career Clarity framework is about addressing the underlying career fulfillment problems and equipping you with a strategy to use over and over again for the rest of your life. It will help you see (and value) your gifts in a new light, differentiate the superficially sexy ideas from the sustainable ones, and feel natural energy in your work again.

Ignoring a strategy for mapping your career moves is a risky decision. While throwing spaghetti at the wall or "falling into" a career path ends up okay for some folks, taking a step in your career without intentionality often leaves you adrift and spinning. There was a good reason you accepted this position, but as the months go on, you start to feel overwhelmed, overworked, underappreciated, or underpaid. And simultaneously, you're feeling frustrated and hopeless because you thought you'd done everything right to get here. If you're feeling nervous because you don't know exactly how or why you got into this mess in the first place, imagine feeling that way every day over the course of the next 20 to 30 years of your career, bouncing like a pinball from job to job, hoping things will get better but not trusting that you're making the best career decisions. Sounds nauseating and frustrating, right?

Now imagine how life would change if you had a strategic plan guiding your professional development. You'd make career decisions with confidence and ease — and know how to judge when the time is right to make a move. You'd start developing strategic relationships before you need them purely because it's (gasp) fun, so job searching will no longer feel like your hair's been set on fire.

To increase your intentionality and vision when making a career shift, the Career Clarity method will guide you through three phases to finding a career that feels like it truly fits you:

- Phase 1: Finding a few strong-fit ideas of what you want next
- Phase 2: Testing to confirm that your dream is dreamy in reality
- Phase 3: Executing on your strategy to make it happen.

Think of this journey like scaling a giant, gorgeous, slightly terrifying mountain — maybe we call it Mount Fulfillment — and you don't have much mountain climbing experience. Your first phase is preparation: finding the mountain you'd like to climb and deciding what you need to pack in your knapsack for your journey. You'll want a good map, a well-calibrated GPS, water, a flashlight, non-perishable snacks... all that good stuff to help you get to the top of the mountain in a healthy, safe way. You'll want to start learning how to read the weather conditions and decide how to plan an initial route. This stage of career pathing requires auditing your current career assets, deciding which of them you want to take on your career journey, and brainstorming the best-fit ideas to pursue.

You'll never scale the mountain if you don't get off your couch, so the next phase has to be testing your desired path. If you planned a route on paper that isn't doable in real life, or you set out and discover, "Ack, there's a giant ravine ahead!" you'll turn back and give up at the first challenge that looks insurmountable. Therefore, we have to approach your career adventure with curiosity, the ability to be nimble, and willingness to adapt to changing terrain. This phase of career mapping requires courage and vulnerable action-taking. Without those traits, you'll always be wondering "what if" about those ideas in the back of your mind or the path not taken.

And then, the last phase is execution, or actually scaling the mountain to the summit. You've got the right tools, you've learned the best strategy, you've tested a route, so now all you have to do is pick up the pace of your hiking. This phase is where you go all in and go all out to achieve your goal: rebranding yourself to match your target sector, developing new relationships, and finessing your interview strategy. It's tempting to skip straight to this phase and jump out on the mountain, but if you skip over the first two phases, this part of career pathing can be the most painful, frustrating, arduous, and time-consuming of all. Don't do that to yourself! Trust the steps of the process, and you'll get the rewards you're looking for.

The reason a heroic climb resonates so deeply in our cultural context is because we can all see ourselves in the unpredictable ups and downs of a journey. You think you've taken the perfect next step in your work and — WHAM — out jumps the next challenge, whether that's a first child, a missed promotion, a sick parent, an abusive boss, or an unexpected cross-country move. But if the protagonist doesn't know where they're trying to go, the only way their story ends up with a fairytale ending is by sheer luck. We don't want to feel like the outcomes of our life and career choices are purely left to chance.

And when it comes to career success, you don't get hit by the luck truck unless you're standing in the middle of the road.

This book will show you an empowered strategy for navigating career choices so you feel fulfilled, happy, and clear. With its help, you can create a legacy you're proud of.

Approaching this journey with a strategic plan makes all the difference — even if we can't plan every step perfectly. With a framework to guide you, you'll know exactly where in the process you've gotten stuck before, and what you need to get back in motion.

The information in the pages that follow won't be enough by itself. The pathway to a career that makes money and makes a difference is embedded within these chapters, but it's up to you to choose to take action and follow it. The story of a real, incredible career adventure isn't written exclusively from a comfortable hammock at base camp.

Former client Aviva took action to change her career story. She was swirling after her California career as a Hollywood casting agent ended when she lost her biggest contract days after her second son was born. She was feeling uncertain but knew she wanted to start fresh and do work that felt more aligned with her values. Through exploring the process for mapping out what's next, she came up with an idea to start an acting instruction business that let her be home with her boys while making five times more than she'd ever thought possible — and hiring employees for that business by year two. Today, Aviva now runs two six-figure businesses from home and spends more time than ever with her sons.

A story like this is possible for you, too. Even if you didn't go to Harvard Business School, marry rich, or have a trust fund. (Goodness knows I didn't!) But you won't get to tell this kind of great career story if you fall into the trap of letting other people's opinions shape your career.

A guidebook like this will help you untether yourself from opinions, assumptions, and fears to find your own way. Use this book like a textbook, a workbook, or even a devotional to guide you each step of the way. There are clarifying questions sprinkled in at strategic points to help you reflect on the concepts and decide how to apply them in your own journey.

If you hope a change is possible for you, if you've heard a tiny voice stirring in your soul whispering that you can't keep doing the same thing for the next 10 years, or if you believe work can be easier and more fun than you ever imagined, you've already taken the first step toward career clarity.

Let's take the next steps together. Navigating the career waters like an expert takes time — and help.

As my friend and fellow coach Cathryn Carruthers often says: "You've got this, and I've got you."

Yours,
Lisa

CHAPTER 1

When Your Work Doesn't Align with Your Values

It's a lot easier to find a job that looks good on the outside than a job that feels good on the inside.

I, unfortunately, know from experience.

A decade ago, I was working in a fancy-looking corporate consulting job in Washington, D.C., mere steps away from the White House. Each day, I'd put on my Nordstrom Rack professional sheath dress (and sensible commute shoes), walk to the nearest Metro stop, take the subway to the office, change my shoes, grab some caffeine, and sit at my row desk in our "award-winning" open office space, ready to lead phone calls with high-paying clients all day long.

In that era, I was working on advocacy and communications campaigns for world-famous brands, traveling to glamorous places like London, Calgary, New York, Toronto, and Jakarta. I had built a reputation as a subject-matter expert in the company, had more vacation time than any of my friends, and was getting opportunities to speak about grassroots mobilization at conferences and networking groups. I was constantly getting face time with company leadership, boosting my promotional opportunities, and was on the fast track to be promoted to the VP level by my 28th birthday.

And yet, no matter how great it looked, it didn't feel right.

I felt guilty. Like I should appreciate what I had more. What was wrong with me that I wasn't satisfied?

I couldn't quite put my finger on what was wrong until the day my grandfather died.

It was a normal Thursday. My phone started to buzz underneath my desk, and I dug around in my giant commuter purse to find it and silence it. But I looked at the caller ID and stopped cold.

You know when you get a phone call, look at the caller name, realize what time of day it is, and know you have to pick up? This was one of those calls.

It was my dad, who pretty much only called me on birthdays, calling me in the middle of a workday. And it was definitely not my birthday.

I grabbed my phone, power walked across the open office to find an unoccupied conference room, and hesitantly pressed the green "answer" button.

As gently as he could, my dad told me that my 94-year-old grandfather had died that morning in Ohio. He said arrangements were being made for a memorial service, if I wanted to fly out and attend.

While I wasn't surprised by the news — living to 94 is a long, rich life — I was still hurting. I numbly floated back to my desk. It was early in the day. I had a lot of time-sensitive work to do and important meetings to attend, so I tried to pull myself together. In that moment, I remember thinking, "The time for feelings is after work."

There was a particularly important-seeming meeting on my calendar for late afternoon that day, too: a private one-on-one conversation with a recently promoted company leader. We'd never met, and she'd requested the meeting. Since we hadn't discussed an agenda, I figured it was a get-to-know-you conversation I could probably muster up enough composure and professionalism to make my way through.

But walking into the meeting, I could tell I wasn't "there." My body was moving into the room, but my brain and heart were both making plans in Ohio.

The leader walked in behind me and sat down. She started by casually asking me how I was doing.

The question broke right through my fake composure, and I felt the tears start to well up in my eyes. With a squeaky, quiet voice, I said, "Uh, not great. I just found out that my grandfather died."

"Oh, I'm so sorry for your loss," she responded. "Please take all the time you need."

"Thanks," I said. The news of the loss was still so fresh, I hardly knew what else to say.

She took a deep breath. "So," she began, "the reason I wanted to have this meeting was because I'd like to put you on a new client. It's a full-time project in my department, and they need someone who can organize and lead it. I know this is outside your wheelhouse, but we need you."

My brain started spinning. I hardly knew her and thought she didn't know anything about me. Being asked to switch teams at work was totally unexpected — I'd never considered leaving my own beloved department and was already busy (and excelling) with a full workload.

"I… uh… well," I stammered, wiping away an errant tear. "I appreciate being given the opportunity, but this isn't really the kind of work I was intending to do here."

That, apparently, was the wrong answer.

"Well, it's not really up to you to just 'choose' not to," she carefully replied.

She paused, giving me an intense look.

"I'm going to need you to tell me within the next 24 hours if you absolutely cannot do this assignment. I've heard good things about you, but you're replaceable."

I couldn't make eye contact. My gaze fell, and I could feel the pricks of painful tears starting to form again. I stared at the floor in front of me, feeling an uncomfortable knot forming in my throat.

I felt scared and stuck — bamboozled by an opportunity I didn't want, with a leader who didn't actually care about me, with no way out. I didn't even have the logistical information I'd need to answer her. The news was so fresh that I wasn't sure when the funeral service was going to be, or if my family would need me to be in Ohio to help take care of the estate.

"Okay," I whispered.

In silence, I pushed back my chair, turned around, and walked out of the meeting. Beelining straight past my desk, I went immediately into the bathroom, sat down in a toilet stall, and promptly started sobbing.

There's nothing quite like feeling as if you're no longer valued as a person at work, but as a unit of human capital.

After the first wave of shock tears poured out of my eyes, I could feel a new sensation erupting: a tsunami of righteous rage. How could someone who said to "take all the time I needed" tell me in the next breath that I had to make a near-instant decision — and that I wasn't actually that valuable to the company?

In that moment of realization, something inside of me snapped.

I thought, *"This place is not worth this. There has got to be a better way to make a living."*

For the first time, I realized there were things in my life that were more important than my career. My work was not my worth, and my worth and humanity were not contingent on my work product either. If a company wasn't going to honor that, they didn't deserve me anymore.

Despite feeling out of alignment with my core values of freedom, family, and meaningful work, my job had stuff going for it that made it hard to leave. I was on a rocket ship zooming up the corporate ladder, which fed my ego. I was making good money, which allowed me to honor my value of financial stability. I was challenged every day, which, as a learning junkie, I loved. Since it spoke to some of my values, I'd felt conflicted about the company and the role for a long time, but always ended up sticking it out another week.

But that moment shifted the sands within me. It made me realize that no matter how nice those perks were, if my core values weren't being met, I needed to leave. I'd never be truly happy or fulfilled at a company that didn't honor my values or treat me humanely. So I gave myself permission to start looking for an escape route out of that job… while also immediately booking my ticket back to Ohio for my grandfather's memorial service.

That very night, after I hopped off the subway and walked home to my shared apartment, I was ready to operationalize my "that's it, I'm out of here" energy. Rage is a great motivator. I threw on sweatpants, hopped onto the couch, fired up my computer, and started searching for new jobs.

After I opened up my laptop and loaded up LinkedIn, the first step was to start figuring out: what did I want to do next? A deceptively simple question. Despite being good at the work, I hadn't loved what I was doing at the consulting firm, and I'd never really invested time thinking about what I'd want to grow into for the next chapter. I knew the things I definitely didn't want again, but wasn't sure what would fit me better. So my initial job searching ideas that night were full of "maybes" and half-baked hypotheses: *"Maybe leaving corporate America will solve things." "Maybe I need to go work for one company whose mission I love so I don't feel like a mercenary every day." "Maybe I'll feel more valued if I get a raise or a new title."*

As I perused the job boards, I found a startup just outside D.C. that sounded right up my alley. I'd be working to give people greater educational opportunities, democratizing access to the most prestigious universities' programs, and making academia flexible and responsive to people's busy lives. It sounded like a dream.

I opened up an online application to the first job at the company that looked like a pretty good fit. Spent hours updating my resume with the right keywords to get past their applicant tracking software and get an opportunity for an interview. After I'd proofread my materials one last time, I pressed "submit," crossed my fingers, and waited.

A week passed, and… nothing.

Like a woman possessed, I was undeterred. I applied online to the next role at the company that seemed like a strong match. Tailored my cover letter and resume to perfection once again. Submitted it mere hours after the job was posted. And, still crickets.

Finally, I thought to myself, *"I'm not going to settle for their silence. I'd be a great fit at this company. I need to up my job search game."*

I knew that tailoring a resume and cover letter wasn't enough to actually differentiate myself from any other candidates, so I decided to play all-out and use more effective job searching tactics (that we'll describe in Phase 3 of this book) to land an interview and a job offer that perfectly fit my salary requirement within a week.

Beyond the sweet, vengeful satisfaction of putting in my notice at the consulting firm and telling that senior leader that I would never tolerate being treated like that ever again, I was on Cloud 9 because this new job looked perfect on paper. They had custom-created a management-level role for me — the first of its kind for the department. It was a nice pay raise, affording me the ability to buy a fancy new car. The office was close to family. I'd be managing multi-million-dollar advertising campaigns each month, which would definitely stretch me beyond the role I'd had at my last gig. And everyone said I'd really impressed them in the job interview, so I felt like I could float right into the job.

The first few weeks were magical. Literally. The company was holding an all-hands meeting in Disney, and, as a new hire, I'd just made the cut and snagged the final plane ticket to Florida.

But after the "new job" sparkle wore off and I was settling into my fifth week at the company, I started wondering if I'd made a terrible mistake. Again.

The role wasn't quite as it had been described. I had the title of manager but didn't manage anyone. I didn't manage any projects either. Instead, I was an analyst, staring at performance metric spreadsheets for 8 hours a day, every single day — and even though I *like* Excel spreadsheets and know my way around a PivotTable, it was too mind-numbing for me. Instead of using my strategic vision and team management capabilities, I was debating how many characters we could include in an ad headline. I was doing the jobs of more senior folks on other marketing teams better than they were, but wasn't able to do my own data crunching job to my boss' satisfaction. Instead of feeling like a sparkly promotion, it felt like a punishment.

The feeling of floundering wasn't even the worst part. The worst part was the team's culture.

The corporate culture was all about social gatherings, holding company-wide parties and shutting down productivity for the day to celebrate major holidays. But this team took the party atmosphere to the next level. There was a lot of drinking — to the point that on a business trip, there was an expectation that the entire group would go out drinking heavily together, with leadership footing the bill. The team was overwhelmingly white dudes, so intoxicated shenanigans would follow these boozy team meetings, including drunken pushup competitions in dress clothes in hotel lobbies and on dirty street sidewalks. Choosing to stay sober or have a night in felt like self-ostracization and career suicide.

It wasn't just the concerning use of alcohol. The higher up someone got on the team, the more disrespectful they seemed to be to their direct reports. The more these supervisors treated their employees like they were idiots — in our open office where everyone could hear — the more they were protected by leadership when complaints were filed about their behavior. This team essentially controlled the company's profitability and was overflowing with twenty-somethings who hadn't learned the full extent of professionalism, respectfulness, or collaboration.

I had a really difficult relationship with a particular director on the team. Her performance was directly contributing to how I was measured, but when our metrics would falter, she wouldn't explain why or how to fix it. She was constantly short with me when I asked her clarifying questions and wouldn't implement any of my ideas. I'd gone to my boss asking for suggestions on how to get what I needed from her so I could meet my performance objectives, and hadn't received helpful suggestions.

One day, my boss pulled us both into a conference room to have a meeting.

"Finally," I thought. *"We can talk about how this relationship isn't working."*

My boss asked her to share why we were having the meeting. In the 12 minutes that followed, she berated me in front of my boss. No requests for a different way of working together. No acknowledgments of how we were playing for the same team and working toward the same goals. Just airing her anger about how my effort to find ways to work together was undermining her authority.

My mouth fell open. I felt my chest tighten. Shame, embarrassment, rage, grief, and betrayal all started washing over me. My boss wasn't standing up for me, this person's disrespectfulness was being empowered, and I'd foolishly believed there was hope for a way we could work better together.

I couldn't hold it together any longer. I started bawling, right there in front of both of them. (Thank goodness this conference room didn't have glass walls.)

In that moment, I realized some of my non-negotiable values had been violated again — but they were different values this time. I had a lot more freedom in this role and was located super close to family, but in my gut, it became clear that if I wasn't feeling respected or treated humanely, the freedom and location didn't matter anymore.

The conflict of seeking out work that better fit some of my values, only to have other values betrayed, was confusing and disorienting.

I felt like Goldilocks on a never-ending search for the perfect bowl of professional porridge: this one tastes too cold, this one is too hot, this one's too toxic. I'd done so many internships in college across different industries and in my twenties had already tried working in nonprofits, consulting, and now at a startup. I felt like a corporate failure, which is a terrifying prospect for someone with decades left in the working world.

The self-doubt and lingering questions crept back in: "*Is there even a 'right' job for me out there? Why couldn't I just figure it out? Was I just acting entitled, foolishly believing that I could have a job where I enjoyed solving problems that were meaningful for me at a company with a healthy culture and in a way that paid me well? Was it possible to feel satisfied in corporate work?*"

I couldn't accept that I'd always been so eager to grow up and finally be an "adult" in the "real world," and was now decidedly arriving at adulthood only to feel overwhelmed, underappreciated, and ready to abandon the pipe dream of doing meaningful work.

I remember thinking, *"If this is what 'adulthood' is, don't sign me up. I don't want it. I refuse to resign myself to being dead in the eyes and becoming a corporate drone for the next few decades. There's got to be another way."*

This persistent belief — that there had to be a better way to work — combined with my desire to avoid re-experiencing the pain in my early career sent me down the path of obsessively researching the drivers of career fulfillment. Life felt far too short to do work for decades on end that dulled my flame. We all deserve to feel lit up and alive in our work!

That realization turned me into a woman on a mission for the next few years: figure out how to crack open these nagging career satisfaction questions to find the joy and keep from experiencing so much anxiety, stress, and pain around work. While I held down that toxic job to keep paying the bills in the short term, I dove deeply into the data about how to finally find the career that fits all your values and needs.

The existing research on career fulfillment wasn't hopeful, at least at first. I realized I wasn't alone in having unsatisfying professional experiences. The first major body of workplace research I discovered, from the Conference Board, joyfully reported that the employee satisfaction data they gathered in 2018 was at a 20-year high... with a whopping 54% of employees feeling "satisfied" by their work.

"Satisfied." That's the bar. And barely more than half of American employees are reaching it.

Job site Monster did a worldwide study of work satisfaction, and the global results are similarly disappointing: Canadians are the highest at 64%, but only 46% of Brits and 43% of the French report loving or strongly liking their work.

Besides crying in the bathroom at work, there are plenty of other consequences for our global dissatisfaction at work. Work unhappiness has the capability to spill over and suck away the joys inside our personal lives, too, if left unchecked.

Maybe you've come home drained and can only muster up enough energy to watch Netflix with a glass of wine.

You definitely don't have the motivation or gas left in the tank to pursue your dream of starting a nonprofit, writing a book, or running a marathon. *"Not right now,"* you tell yourself. Maybe you're noticing that you're coping with your dissatisfying day job in other ways: skipping morning workouts in favor of pulling the covers back up over your head. Or desperately relying on intense physical activity every day to let off steam and frustration. Feeling sluggish. Having a couple extra mimosas (or doughnuts, or hits of weed) at brunch to take the edge off. Avoiding confrontational conversations. Yelling at your kids after work for something trivial when you didn't mean to but couldn't stop yourself. Watching your phone's average screen time report slowly creep up, week after week.

How we feel about our work has the possibility to seep into and infect every other part of our lives.

Can you imagine what our world would look like if people enjoyed — nay, even loved — their work?

We would have more energy. Studies show that doing work you're good at and that you enjoy gives you energy instead of sucking it away. More energy means more productivity within our jobs, more capacity to give to family and friends outside of work. We'd feel motivated to exercise or play with our kiddos or write our first novel after work because we'd still have gas left in the tank.

We'd perform better because we'd care more. Research shows that performance at work improves by anywhere from 12-36% when you like your work and feel your contributions make a difference. Better performance usually means more promotions, raises, eligibility for bonuses, additional challenging responsibilities, and higher job security.

We would also be happier. As Elle Woods, the unlikely lawyer from *Legally Blonde* brilliantly stated in her client's court defense: "Happy people just don't shoot their husbands." There are a lot of things genuinely happier people don't do as often, like numb out with alcohol, drugs, or other coping substances. Consistently happier people have more emotional resilience to weather the challenges of life and often extend more empathy and compassion to others who are struggling.

Our lives might even feel more meaningful. One of the biggest predictors of mental health and fulfillment across studies is a sense of groundedness and meaning in your life: you feel like your life is purposeful and you exist for a reason. The data tends to show that the healthiest, most stable individuals have a deep sense of spiritual connection to purpose in their lives. Work that validates or enhances a sense of meaning, purpose, and impact can legitimately improve the quality of our lives.

By reading this book, you are taking a step toward creating this more energized, happy, meaningful world. That's why this career pathing work lights my soul on fire: it creates a life improvement ripple effect both within you and far beyond you.

As an example, there were certainly positive ripples from Julia's career change. Julia was a special education teacher in inner city Chicago, and she needed to get out of teaching. As much as she was passionate about her work and loved the impact she made, the lifestyle and stress weren't a fit for her bigger dreams of traveling and serving bigger communities. After moving through the Career Clarity process, Julia transitioned from education into a program manager role at a nonprofit that allowed her work to have local and global impact, and even allowed her to bring a friend with her to travel abroad each year on the company dime. Finding a job that's in alignment with your values, empowers you to live out your travel dreams, and increases your ability to understand and empathize with other cultures is a great ripple.

Or, your wave might look similar to the one Matt created. He worked in a sector that most people covet: international development. He'd worked his ass off to get into the field but was feeling like his growth, impact, and earning potential had all stalled. Matt felt disconnected from what he liked or even who he was, and was phoning it in at work. That stale energy started to trickle into his marriage and into his workouts, leaving him feeling less alive. Through reconnecting with his values and the areas in which he wanted to grow, Matt made the transition into a joyful role supporting nonprofits with their growth and development from the private sector, while also nurturing his dream to add more writing back into his life.

Notice that each of these stories is wildly different. Each person who walks through the Career Clarity process defines values and success on their own terms.

My mission is to show underfulfilled people that life is too short to work a job that doesn't light you up — and if you're willing to explore what success means for you, there's a real-deal framework to find work that will ignite you and fulfill you at every stage of your career.

Ready to learn the framework to successfully climb to your career summit?

Here's one more tool to put into your toolbox for the journey ahead: since all the supplemental resources I wanted to share with you wouldn't fit into one book alone, go to GetCareerClarity.com/Bonus to download free bonus companion worksheets, along with a few other surprise goodies to stay organized and focused along your journey.

CHAPTER 2

A Framework for Successful Career Changes

From seeing thousands of smart, capable people who were stuck and didn't know how to find fulfillment, it was clear this journey needed a defined method to show you where to begin and how to progress through the steps. This framework is organized into three core phases that mirror the key stages of the career transition process.

Phase 1 focuses on identifying who you are and what you value most. Much of the standard career advice starts by trying to figure out market demand: what kind of jobs already exist on job boards and how hard would it be to fit yourself into those roles? But an approach that starts with thinking about the employer's needs before your own is a surefire way to miss out on fulfillment (or stumble upon it by accident). It isn't that the employer's needs aren't important — this book will not teach you to act like an entitled snot in the workplace — but when you start prioritizing their needs before considering your own, you never give fulfillment a fighting chance. That means the first goal is to get clear on what your non-negotiable values are and use those prioritized needs to brainstorm the kinds of work that might best fit you. There's a specific process for this, using a methodology I developed over the years called the 4 Pillars of Career Fulfillment that you'll explore in depth in Chapters 8 through 11.

If you walk through each of the steps in Phase 1, by the end you'll have a couple strategic, thorough, thoughtful hypotheses about the work that fits your personal definition of a fulfilling career. Phase 1 leaves you feeling excited and certain about the value of your gifts. Instead of feeling stuck, overwhelmed, or blank, you'll feel motivated, focused, and full of promising possibilities for what's next.

The ideas by themselves aren't enough, so that's where we move into Phase 2. This phase is where we take your future career ideas out for a test drive. Phase 2 of your career expedition is something most people would prefer to skip over, because it slows things down and requires you to dip your toes into the water of a future career, instead of jumping in with reckless abandon.

However, that's what makes Phase 2 critically important: it defines the distinction between the dream of a career and the actual, experiential reality. An idea for your future job might seem perfect on paper, but you don't get to live the "paper" version. You have to live in the real, day-to-day one. And this one is what you need to be intimately familiar with before committing to your new career path: the version that isn't as glossy, that has real pros and cons.

I can't tell you the number of people I've worked with who got a graduate degree thinking that the dream of being a therapist, a teacher, an accountant, a lawyer, whatever would "fix" their career dissatisfaction. They didn't test drive the work in reality quite enough before applying to grad school, and by the time they graduated and were a few months into this career "fix," they felt sheer terror. Discovering you don't want to do the work your degree qualifies you to do but not knowing where to go next (while swimming in hundreds of thousands of dollars of student loan debt) isn't the reality I want for you. By taking a big risk like switching jobs or starting graduate school without having sufficiently validated your path, you can end up stuck or severely limited in the immediate viability of alternative career options. This financial burden is why so many people think a career change is permanently out of reach. However, even if you have student loan debt, no career pivot is off the table forever if you come up with a risk-managed strategy to try it.

The most risk-managed testing approach will include a series of small-scale experiments to gather more information, answer looming questions, and get a taste of what the work is like before you take the bigger leap. By the time you've successfully completed Phase 2, you'll have clarity, confidence, and plenty of experiential data points that validate the kind of work that *actually* fits you so you can go all in (and all out) on your job search.

Playing "all out" is the energy and mindset of Phase 3. The third phase is where you take all the preparation and information and apply it to change your career and life. This is the part where you "go for it."

As you start Phase 3, you'll thank your past self for doing the intensive self-reflection and groundwork in Phases 1 and 2. That introspection and testing means now you know what work will work for your life right now. You've built strategic relationships in your target industry, you know the key players in the sector, and you have a sense of not only the role you want to step into but the career paths that role would open up for you.

Phase 3 is where you translate your newfound knowledge, clarity, and confidence from Phases 1 and 2 into proof for hiring managers, which is all about being savvy about your branding and positioning as a candidate. The goal is to market yourself in a way that feels non-slimy and non-sleazy, a way that feels authentic, credible, and (dare I say) fun. Marketing yourself as your target organization's dream hire requires two parts: telling your professional story powerfully and getting the right people to open doors for you.

From strategic relationships to new frameworks for ensuring your professional brand is on fire for interviewing and negotiating strategically, you'll have all the tactics and resources you need to make your transition as easily, quickly, and successfully as possible. Go all in and all out, and, by the end of Phase 3, you will have not only successfully secured a job doing work that suits you and that you adore, but you will also have developed skills and relationships that can serve you throughout the rest of your life. Not too shabby.

The three phases encompass a lot of sequential steps and processes. That's on purpose: there's a big difference between just getting a new job... and making your career transition a joyful, fulfilling one.

You deserve to upgrade your life, not just trade one job for another with the "same BS, different day." That's a lesson I learned firsthand in the first few years after becoming a career coach.

When I first started coaching, I'd assumed once I helped someone transition into their new job, they'd be set for life. I'd send them on their merry way, rainbows and confetti would burst forth on their first day at the new organizations, and life would be perfect forevermore.

Several years ago, I was sitting at my computer when an email popped in from Jaime, a former client.

I got excited. I love getting updates! Last time we spoke, Jaime had transitioned from working for her family business to being a Jane-of-all-trades at a children's advocacy nonprofit.

I settled in with a steaming mug of English breakfast tea and started reading what I thought was going to be a gushing note. Maybe it would be about how much she loved her employer, how she's been growing, or even news about a recent promotion or raise.

And, holy crap, was I wrong.

Embarrassment crept in as I read how Jaime, who had accepted this new job seeking work she felt passionately about, was working way too many hours and suffering physical consequences of stress and overwork. Jaime was working loads of overtime hours, seeing recurring health issues flare back up, and was so unhappy that she was already interviewing for new jobs less than a year after we'd worked together. I felt embarrassed and guilty that her situation hadn't been the perfect fit.

Then, the day got worse.

Another email. This time from Deja. (Remember Deja from the Introduction? She was the American ex-pat living in London.) When we'd last spoken, she'd successfully networked and hustled into a dream job running live events in Europe for a world-famous health and wellness brand. In her update, Deja told me that her dream job wasn't turning out to be quite so dreamy. She'd initially prioritized getting a job that fit her

Lifestyle needs and allowed her to take fitness classes anytime she wanted. But she'd come to realize that her real priority was working with a team full of creative, compassionate humans she adored. So Deja was in the process of interviewing for another job, too!

I was crushed and ashamed. I'd been using models and research to guide them into their new jobs, but they clearly weren't sustainably happy. Was I failing my clients?

Both women were delighted to get back in touch, were glad to share their updates, and sounded incredibly positive about the changes they were navigating. They didn't harbor any blame or resentment because their employment situations were shifting again. They actually seemed excited to be taking the reins in their transitions again.

Even though they were unhappy, they'd both learned more nuance about who they were, what they prioritized most, and how to translate general career satisfaction principles to their specific situations. They were writing to share how they'd used the skills developed through our work to do something about their dissatisfaction, instead of floundering or letting their work situations spiral out of control. Instead of years of angst, they were reporting a few months in a poor-fit role that became a springboard into something even better.

Jaime and Deja felt empowered because they understood their own prioritized fulfillment formulas and trusted they could find more satisfying work. By taking action, they'd each discovered their critically important culture and lifestyle values when it comes to happy work.

It was a theme popping up with more and more of my clients: while we can analyze everything we want in our next jobs, if we don't understand and prioritize those desires on a personal level, we end up in a cycle carrying old baggage and dissatisfaction from the last job right on into the new one, and never find the transcendent, fulfilling work we're after.

I learned a lot about prioritization from Jaime and Deja, and made a clear prioritization process one of the philosophical underpinning of the Career Clarity framework and this book. Because you need — and deserve — a guidebook showing you how to take all the differing models and properly prioritize and apply them in your own life. So think of this book like your personal career trail map. But not a shiny, hot-off-the-press, unused terrain map you'd pick up at the park entrance. You deserve a well-worn, tried-and-true map with secret trails, viable shortcuts, cautionary warnings, and areas for exploration all labeled. Think of Harry Potter and his trusty Marauder's Map, and how much easier your career exploration could be with a living, dynamic document full of helpful hints around every corner. You won't find your fulfilling career following a generic set of steps and definition of success, so you need an expansive framework with clear guiding principles to lead you towards the path that best fits you. Your own professional road less traveled.

For some people, this process will help them discover that their current job is actually a pretty good fit, but changing a couple key pieces would make it an outstanding one. For others, they'll realize why their current job has felt so crappy for so long because they can now clearly see the sort of work their soul's naturally meant to be doing. And for others, there's a moment of realization that the road toward entrepreneurship is the ideal fit. No matter which of these different trails best matches your heart and soul's needs, this book has the tools to help you get there.

To start charting the ideal path for you, let's explore how you'll figure out what you really, really want by preparing you for Phase 1.

CHAPTER 3

Mapping the Drivers of a Fulfilling Career

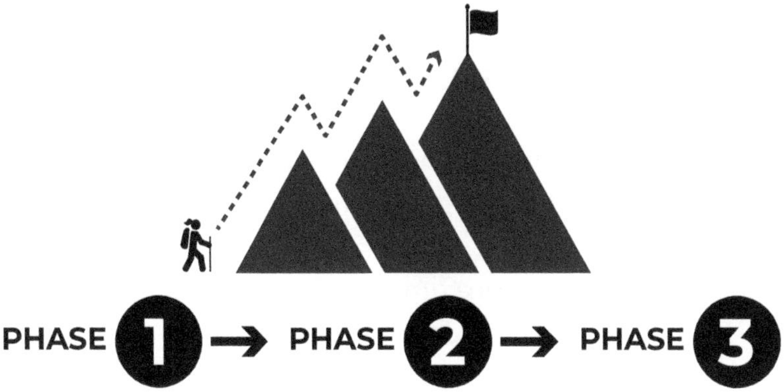

If someone asked you to define the exact components of the most fulfilling career for you, what would you say?

Some of my clients would feel totally stumped and embarrassed, and mumble something like: “I don’t know… yet.” Others might name a few core values but then worry their answers aren’t “good enough” or sound like the same generic things everyone else says they want: a steady paycheck, good colleagues, decent health insurance. Others secretly wish they could just flip the bird and walk away from the question completely.

If you don't have a bullet-pointed list of qualities at the ready, you aren't alone. Chances are your education never included a study of how to find work that fulfills you. Societally, we don't focus on teaching individuals how to identify (or create) a juicy, energizing career path.

But that's not to say that a framework for finding fulfilling work doesn't exist, or is as believable as unicorns or Bigfoot.

The component parts of life-giving work are both universal and deeply personal, which makes them tough to teach in a social media-worthy soundbite. And even more important: they're part of an iterative process you'll learn throughout the pages of this book.

There's existing data on common themes among satisfied workers across the world, but it isn't always helpful: the takeaways from the ivory tower white papers can feel so broad, generalized, and static that they seem impossible to actually apply.

Take the nonprofit organization 80,000 Hours, an amazing institution which has been responsible for loads of analysis on meaningful work over the last decade. Their deep dive into the research on job satisfaction identified six factors that drive contentedness: work you're good at, work that helps others, work that's engaging, having supportive colleagues, no major negatives, and fit with the rest of your personal life.

The research is helpful context, but it's tough to make this model feel personal enough to use: *"What does "supportive" look like to me? Doesn't all work help others somehow?"* The trick to taking big, ambiguous research questions and creating a framework that's a perfect mix of personal and universal is to define the concepts for yourself.

After watching the trends emerging from hundreds of happy and fulfilled career changers year over year, I started to notice there were four consistent drivers of work satisfaction that every happy employee needs to know. I named them the 4 Pillars of Career Fulfillment.

Here's a brief summary of each pillar. We'll explore each pillar in depth together in the following chapters.

The first pillar of career fulfillment is **Strengths**, defined as the things you can do and learn to do that you enjoy and get energy from. If you aren't working in a role where you get to use your unique gifts to make a difference for your organization, the likelihood's high you won't feel completely fulfilled. We'll be careful not to make the cardinal mistake of thinking your capabilities are your strengths, and will pay specific attention to your potential, momentum, and intrinsic motivation. Strengths will help us see the ideal responsibilities and professional growth opportunities for you. As we mentioned in Chapter 2, prioritization is a key piece of this framework, so consider if the specific job duties you perform tend to be a big factor into whether you enjoy the work. If that's true, Strengths might be your highest priority pillar.

The second pillar of fulfillment is **Magnetic Interests**. Your interests are the kinds of topics, problems, and people that you're magnetically attracted toward and would choose to spend free time exploring. For some people, this is the most important part of a job. This might be you if you find yourself obsessively searching for job openings for brands or causes that speak to your soul. (You would also never consider working for a company that's not 100% aligned with your values, and you may often have strong opinions or tend to think in black-and-white.) For others, the goal is simply to work on something you're curious about, not necessarily putting all your "passion" eggs into one work basket.

The third pillar driving career satisfaction is **Personality**, or the innate way you're wired to look at the world, make decisions, and organize your time. Each of us is blessed with a slightly different personality, and your personality is one of the biggest factors that determines whether or not an organization is going to be a good cultural fit for you. If you're an introvert who's worked in an extroverted environment or a planner who has worked in a workplace designed for spontaneity and flexibility, you may have already felt discomfort between who you naturally are and who the job is asking you to be. For Deja, personality was definitely out of whack. She craves a supervisor who loves her, "gets" her, and constantly pushes her to keep growing — and while her last job was incredibly impressive, her managers weren't setting her up for success or sustainability.

The final pillar of career fulfillment is **Lifestyle**. The purpose of work in your life is not just to make the time that you spend earning money more joyful and valuable to you, but to also to give you the resources and the energy to create a life you love outside of work, too. If your work gets in the way of things that are important to you, like relationships, your health, your hobbies, or your downtime, the job is likely not a good fit for you. This is where things like a long commute, a requirement to be present in the office five days a week, or bosses who judge your contributions by the number of hours they see you in your desk chair can bite you. Jaime's Lifestyle pillar was all wrong. The nonprofit expected her to work a minimum of 50-hour weeks, and because she was carefully managing some health conditions, it was setting her up for a huge crash.

The 4 Pillars of Career Fulfillment framework is the reason why you can be in a job that looks like a good fit on the outside but doesn't quite feel like it fits you, or why a job that looks like a "dream job" on paper can feel like a nightmare in real life. You can have three out of the four pillars in good shape, but that last one could be tainting your sense of satisfaction. The overlap point between your strengths, magnetic interests, personality, and lifestyle is as unique to you as your fingerprint. Identifying these for yourself and using them like a rubric to grade potential future opportunities allows you to stop picking roles that seem "sexy" on the outside, and to find roles that are juicy, life-giving, and a strong fit for the nuance of who you are.

The pillars each have lots of components within them. The goal isn't to find a perfect glass slipper "dream job" because the idea of one singular "right" job across every single possible dimension is a fairytale. Instead, the goal is to understand what you value most within each of these four categories, and then prioritize within and across each pillar. Not every pillar carries the same weight for each person, and distinguishing your top priority pillar is imperative to identify what work will fit you.

Within each pillar, there will be non-negotiable things you need, as well as things you want. It's important to identify the "nice-to-haves" so they don't end up distracting from your deepest needs. This might mean you have to trade things that are externally shiny and tempting for the things that are critical to your personal happiness equation. Understanding that you aren't shooting for perfectly getting every single thing on your list, but instead strategically making a tradeoff to be satisfied with your non-negotiables, helps to focus the way you'll apply the tools in the coming pages.

It's also important to remember that the prioritization of your needs and pillars changes with time and experience. What you wanted at 23 is different from what you'll crave at 46, because of both who you've already been and who you're becoming. Defining each pillar is not something you should do once and assume you're set for life: you should expect to dynamically revisit each pillar periodically and make adjustments to course-correct your next steps. For help in identifying your current top priority pillar, head to GetCareerClarity.com/Bonus to take a free fulfillment driver assessment.

When you follow this framework, you can get crystal clear on your non-negotiable needs, ideal priorities, and the things you will not tolerate so you can calibrate your internal GPS and zero in on companies and jobs that will create a more delightful career.

In the coming chapters, we'll dive into each of the 4 Pillars so you can see where you're in alignment or where you might need to make some adjustments. But before we do, here's the warning sign at the beginning of your climb up Mount Fulfillment: the path to a fulfilling career isn't a yellow brick road. In fact, it's not paved at all, which means we need to train you to look out for loose rocks or potential avalanche conditions before you start your expedition.

That means our journey through Phase 1 actually begins with recalibrating your awareness and your mindset.

CHAPTER 4

The Mindsets that Help You Get Unstuck

By now, it's clear there's a big difference between a successful, happy career changer and a person who bounces from mediocre job to job: it's following a systematic process instead of throwing spaghetti at the wall. But there's another difference that can prevent you from making a constructive transition and implementing the steps of the process successfully.

That difference is knowing — and mastering — your psychology.

Most career resources talk ad nauseum about strategies and tactics for making your move, but few address the underlying mindsets and beliefs that set you up for success (or failure) from the get-go. So, before you get to the tactical execution, you have to get your mind right. That means knowing and adopting the most helpful strategy and attitudes. Each of the 4 Pillars will be more effective and helpful for you if we establish strong self-awareness and helpful mindsets as a baseline.

Even the highest performing, smartest people who try to take action on all the information they consume will fail to reach their goals if they don't address problematic underlying belief systems. Your innermost thoughts have an insane amount of control over your results.

> “If [more] information was the answer, then we'd all be billionaires with perfect abs.
>
> Derek Sivers

One of the beliefs that can sabotage your career transition is the idea that you don't like, can't handle, or don't want to feel pain. Why are your thoughts about pain so critical? The thing that separates the people who do endless research into information online about a future career change from the people who push themselves to get uncomfortable, recalibrate their beliefs, and take massive action is usually pain.

Think about the pain-action connection like this: if you're a little under the weather, but not running a serious fever or feeling nauseous, are you likely to go to the doctor? Probably not. You might take a sick day from work, but your behavior won't change more than taking it easy and possibly popping a vitamin.

But if you're running to the bathroom every 20 minutes or your fever spikes dramatically, are you going to get your butt into an Urgent Care, stat? Probably so.

There's a physical or emotional pain threshold that pushes us from tolerating into acting.

At work, it's the difference between the emotional pain of thinking, *"Oh, bummer, guess I have to work with that unpleasant team again"* and thinking, *"There is NO way I am going to tolerate being disrespected and undermined by that team every day for the next year."*

More pain leads to a higher commitment to taking the meaningful steps needed to kickstart a change.

If you haven't reached your pain threshold, this book can give you all the information in the world, but it won't help you change your situation. In order to create lasting change, the first thing you need to do to set yourself up for success is to *let yourself feel the full pain about your current situation.*

It's not enough to recognize that there is pain, because so many of us have spent huge chunks of our lives seeing and then trying to avoid pain by glossing over things, minimizing them, or ignoring them. While those avoidant choices can be adaptive in some situations, they also directly contribute to feeling stuck if we lean on them too much. Another crutch can be choosing to "numb out" our feelings, using exercise, food, excessive research, alcohol, weed, or YouTube to distract us and replace our feelings with different, quieter sensations. Sensations that may make us forget that leaving is actually an option.

The more we make choices that let us hide from the pain we're feeling, the more we allow ourselves to stay stuck.

Think about the implications: the more we numb out, the more we enable our current painful situation to continue unchecked. While numbing out is normal and societally accepted, if we press the "mute" button on our pain and let it live another day, the pain will never reach the threshold where we have to take action.

Remember when my boss told me she was sympathetic to my loss but I needed to get back to work after my grandfather passed? That was the heart-wrenchingly awful push I needed to hit my personal pain threshold. It's no coincidence I went into a rage and applied for jobs like a hellion that very same night.

The first step to using your painful feelings as motivational fire is to identify them and name them. On its face, this process might seem too simple to be a helpful starting point. However, slowing down to feel the nuances and depth of every emotion work brings up is important to avoid accidentally making similar mistakes again.

If you let yourself really feel your pain and understand the consequences of continuing on this path, it becomes far easier to commit to taking action. And one thing that usually comes hand-in-hand with commitment is more comfort with experiencing the extremes of the emotions about your work.

When I say "extreme," I mean it. There's a wide range of emotions that can bubble up, from grief to red-hot rage.

Career transitions can be especially painful because they're tied to the pain of loss: loss of the idealized dream of the job, loss of the identity that work had symbolized, loss of the hope that things might get better on their own. Because of that, we can use the five stages of grief to help you dig deeper into the experiences you've had at work and the corresponding emotions they've dredged up.

> "I did not know that I was supposed to feel everything. I thought I was supposed to feel happy. I thought that happy was for feeling and that pain was for fixing and numbing and deflecting and hiding and ignoring. I thought that when life got hard, it was because I had gone wrong somewhere. I thought pain was weakness and that I was supposed to suck it up. But the thing was that the more I sucked it up, the more food and booze I had to suck down.
>
> Glennon Doyle, *Untamed*

Here's a refresher on how the typical Introduction to Psychology class defines the five emotion and feeling stages of grief: you've got denial, anger, bargaining, depression, and acceptance.

As you read through the description of the Five Stages of Career Grief below, notice how many of the stages of grief have you seen yourself in. These stages aren't linear — you don't neatly move from one to the next — so you'll probably notice you've felt all, several, or just one of these as you've been wrestling with your career. If you're currently in the thick of the grief stages in your work right now, you may continue to bounce back and forth between several before arriving at acceptance and hope.

Grab some paper and a pen or open your favorite digital note-taking platform to jot down some thoughts on what hits home most for you across these possible emotional states. Don't hold back: every dissatisfaction data point you can collect is going to be part of the push to transform your emotional pain into activated momentum. Yes, even if you've taken the Myers-Briggs personality assessment, scored as an INTJ, and are secretly hoping you don't have any emotions around work. You will see something that resonates here. (Hint: Try looking for anger.)

Shock, Disbelief, and Denial

Shock is the moment you get caught completely off guard by something awful happening at work: you're pulled off a project you loved and put on a project you hate. Your coworker — whose job you've been doing for the last year and a half — gets promoted and you don't. There's a re-organization of your department, and you're assigned to a new team where there aren't any leaders in leadership. Your beloved boss is fired, and it's clear you're probably next on the chopping block. Shock tends to kick in because your nervous system has been completely surprised and goes into "freeze" mode instead of fight or flight. It's as if your usual coping mechanisms are paralyzed, and all you can do is watch someone publicly blame and berate you for a mistake that *they* made, your mouth agape.

Disbelief and denial are what happen after your body kicks back into action post-shock, saying, *"There's no way she just called me incompetent in front of everyone right now."* They're defense mechanisms that reject reality and pretend something didn't happen so your brain can keep you psychologically safe and you don't have to relive the experience. If someone stole your idea, badmouthed you, spread misinformation about your performance, or yelled at you in a meeting, disbelief is choosing not to accept the facts because it would be too painful and frustrating to acknowledge it. Denial can look like not telling anybody about your experience, refuting that it ever happened, or saying that it wasn't a big deal (when it clearly was a Big Deal). If you've ever thought or said comments like these, you may have experienced denial:

> *"I mean, nobody's happy all the time in their work, right?"*
>
> *"I'm not really drinking a bottle of wine (or using edibles) tonight because I resent my job…"*
>
> *"It wasn't really as bad as it sounds…"*
>
> *"My boss only made misogynistic/racist/anti-Semitic/etc. comments once or twice… they probably just meant it to lighten the mood."*

Denial can be temporarily helpful if you have no spare emotional bandwidth to process what happened (or if your work environment is unsafe), but it's not a healthy tool to use long term.

Anger

Anger is an incredibly important emotion because people who get mad take action. Anger's one of the quickest and most powerful ways to elicit immediate change from yourself or others.

Anger is often called the emotion of justice: it tends to appear when your beliefs or values have been violated, like if you've started to notice things being handled wrong at work, or a coworker being disrespected by a client and you're fed up with it.

> “The person who is angry at the right things and toward the right people, and also in the right way, at the right time and for the right length of time is morally praiseworthy.
>
> Aristotle

While it's an uncomfortable emotion, anger has an adaptive, survival-based purpose: it's a visceral, bodily signal that something needs to change.

The physiological experience of anger is just as important as the psychological one. You don't just “think” you're angry, you feel it. Subtle bodily changes can include elevated heart rate, quickness of breath, increases in blood pressure, clenched jaw, muscle tension, or a furrowed brow. This is your body's way of physically preparing you to take immediate action — it's not meant to be your new normal for months or years on end. Looking for symptoms of low-level stewing anger is useful if you have strong emotional control and might have a hard time identifying intense emotions around work. Just follow your physiological signs. They won't lie.

Anger can be useful when it's righteous indignation that prompts you to take action on your own behalf, like when you were passed over for a project and immediately whipped up a bullet point-laden, 11-page slide deck of the ways you'd kick ass at it.

But there are plenty of ways anger can be problematic in the workplace instead of a vehicle for justice and change. It can be seen as a sign of "losing control" or being overly emotional. Displays of anger that don't reflect emotional maturity can be rageful and destructive (like slamming a door or swearing at someone) or silent and manipulative (like ignoring someone's contributions or icing them out in a meeting).

While we don't want to artificially limit our emotional spectrum to only express socially acceptable feelings, some explosive manifestations of anger aren't effective at changing your circumstances. However, internalizing or suppressing all your anger has harmful negative physical, emotional, and mental consequences — and staying in an angering professional situation only compounds those painful consequences.

Bargaining and Guilt

The bargaining stage is the most devastating part of the career grief cycle, because here you start playing incredibly unhelpful mind games with yourself. When you're bargaining, you'll make seemingly rational but completely outlandish statements like:

> *"If I can only get a $10,000 raise at the next review, I'll be happy."*

> *"I could have done a better job on that last report, so I deserve this happening to me, and maybe when I make a report more perfect, I'll get the accolades I deserve."*

> *"If I can just survive here another 2 years here, I'll get my pension/have that deal close/make partner and then I can leave."*

> *"Being berated in front of my colleagues must be my fault because I did a bad job. I'll do a better job next time so that won't happen again."*

This mode of thinking is hyper-logical and pushes your happiness out beyond the foreseeable time horizon: *"If I just suffer even more, somehow everything will change and this will all be worth it."* You're trading away your agency today and praying to a magical corporate fairy godmother to bibbidy-bobbity-boop a better career situation onto you in the future.

You bargain because you feel guilty or even responsible for what's happened to you, and negotiating is your penance. (For penance, you might be better off with three Hail Marys and two Our Fathers.) It often seems easier to strike a short-term bargain instead of making bigger long-term changes to your career or life.

Bargaining makes you believe you can solve past pains by making a deal about what fresh hell you'll tolerate in the future. It's settling disguised as hope.

When you're trading what you want now for what you think you can get later, look out. To most companies, you are a unit of human capital that is valuable but interchangeable — and easily replaceable, if needed. When you're in a bad situation but negotiate with yourself to justify staying, you usually end up losing even more. Unless there's a clear, time-bound plan with a light at the end of the tunnel, like your employer reimbursing your grad school tuition if you stay six more months and you're setting better boundaries to make those months workable, bargaining will only lead you back into more grief.

Depression

Feeling sad about your job situation sucks. There's no way around that. It isn't called "career grief" for nothing.

But letting yourself acknowledge — and feel — the depth of your sadness is a great way to clear those emotions out and keep the feelings from consuming you forever.

(An ugly cry in the bathroom between meetings to try to "keep it all together" does not count. Nor does becoming Debbie Downer or Moaning Myrtle every night after you get home.)

Pay attention to feeling sadness within the container of work.

"I'm incredibly disappointed that this company I admired doesn't share my values" is a totally different flavor than a never-ending fountain of misery about who you are and your lot in life, like *"I'll never be happy in any job. Anywhere. Ever."*

There's a distinction between useful sadness and chronic, self-shaming, catastrophized thinking -- taking your specific circumstances and generalizing them out to all possible work scenarios. Catastrophized, black-and-white, "always" and "never" thinking isn't productive or healthy. It's usually symptomatic of slipping into a fixed mindset (*"I always mess things up at work"*) or a streak of perfectionistic thinking (*"I can't stop until I've found the one right job for me"*), both of which cause you more suffering than the situation actually requires.

Acceptance and Hope

Acceptance gets a bad reputation because it sounds like you're choosing to settle for your current reality. But in the context of career grief, acceptance is a return to hopefulness because you're no longer denying what's really going on.

Instead of "it is what it is" (which could be denial-based or depression-based thinking), acceptance is shifting your mindset to "*I see what it is, and I see what I can and can't do about it.*"

There's a lot of power in this mindset evolution. Your dream of how this job could be great has died, but now that you've accepted its demise, you're free to pursue a new path that fits you better. You can learn from your last work situation and use it to inform how you choose your next job or career.

Acceptance is not always easy or fun to get to, but it's totally possible. It's certainly the most forward-looking place to be in your career grief cycle.

I know emotional identification work isn't the fun part of exploring new careers. However, if you skip over this step and read the rest of the chapters, you might realize you never took a single action because you were too bogged down in avoiding the feels. If you're taking the time to read this in your busy life and truly are craving a change, find a way to put in the extra few minutes to apply as much as you can as you go.

This is your official permission to let it out: let the tears spill out about the injustice around never getting credit for your amazing ideas, or how frustrating it is to get passed over for that promotion again. Rage about all the times you worked late without so much as a "thank you." Feel the regret or guilt about bargains you've struck in the past that kept you stuck and miserable.

When my boss asked me to jump right back into work after my grandfather died, I experienced a lot of emotions all at once: frustration that I wasn't being treated like a human, and terror in thinking about quitting. I was mad at myself for not already having the "perfect" career, and bargaining about how I could still patch it back together. Trying to sweep that emotional experience under the rug might have led to months or years of extra suffering in a job that was wildly out of alignment. Identifying the elements of career grief saved me from unnecessary additional suffering.

As you read through these stages, you might have wondered, *"Why don't I write down the happy times, too?"* Here's the rationale: your brain is either going to naturally try to surface the happy thoughts as its own coping mechanism, effectively blunting the intense, painful emotions that are coming up, or it's going to ignore the happy moments completely and really lean into the sadness, fear, and anger until you have a breakthrough moment and decide you won't tolerate this crap anymore.

Now that you've identified the feelings you've experienced in the past, we need to turn up the volume on them for the future. We won't leave you in this wallowing emotional state forever — in fact, the entire 4 Pillars methodology is built on identifying the delightful things that leave you feeling happy and fulfilled — but we need you to feel the full power of your feelings now so the rest of this work is effective for you. Nothing can sabotage a promising new career like avoiding processing your emotions about the old one.

> If you're noticing your thoughts tend to stay in the "no light at the end of the tunnel" space as you walk through this reflective exercise, this process isn't meant to replace the help of a qualified therapist in processing these experiences and emotions. Seek out a listening ear, whether it's a mentor, therapist, or spiritual counselor to help you if you're getting bogged down in revisiting these feelings. (And while your employer might be the problem, lots of companies offer confidential Employee Assistance Programs with free or reduced-cost therapy that could support you as you're creating your exit plan.)

Minimization or numbing out make it hard to feel pain, so to fully activate any of the emotions that came up for you, the clarifying questions outlined at the end of this chapter will put the feelings in a bigger context. Sit with the reflections about what you've felt at work in the past, and how you'd rather feel instead, like: *"What are the consequences of staying in your current situation longer?"* Or, *"What does tolerating this situation say about my values?"*

Each of these "intensifying" questions has a subtext: how would you rather feel, moving forward, on a daily basis? The questions are asking for your full-hearted commitment to take action and change your situation. Conviction that your future joy is worth fighting for.

If you're fully committed to taking real action and no longer numbing out, you're making big progress on managing and mastering your mindset here. Let's keep going: there are a few more ways to prepare your mind and heart before you start applying the Career Clarity model.

CLARITY QUESTIONS:

What are the emotional and opportunity consequences if you minimize or numb out and wait to take action for another year? Five years?

How is choosing not to take action causing you extra pain and violating your values? (Pain can be physical, emotional, financial, or even wasted resources like time or energy, etc.)

Who else is suffering because you're allowing yourself to stay stuck in your current work situation? Your partner? Your friends? Your children? Your community?

If you stay in this job, what does that say about your priorities and values? What kind of example is that setting for your current or future children, nieces and nephews, etc.?

CHAPTER 5

Taking Action Even When You're Unsure

The next element of understanding and working with your psychology might be even harder than letting yourself get emotional about work. It's recognizing that successfully making a change in your work requires you to feel your fear and take action anyway.

Fear is not a sexy starting place for a heroic mountain climbing journey. A lot of people believe you have to start with confidence before taking action and setting out on your trek. While it's a compelling argument, it's backwards: confidence is typically a *byproduct* of taking action, not the cause.

Courageous commitment — the willingness to take action in the face of fear and uncertainty — creates confidence. Not the other way around.

You have to be committed and courageous enough to be an uncertain, messy, ungraceful beginner in order to practice enough times to become a confident, competent master. While it would probably be far more convenient to make fear eat your dust, we can't skip over the courage step and make you fearless, no matter how many toxic positivity self-help articles claim otherwise.

Biologically and scientifically, it's impossible to make you feel fearless unless we lobotomize you. Seriously. Google it. Or, maybe don't Google it. Every member of the animal kingdom, from fish to puppies to you, has a critical brain structure that activates its fear and stress response when a stimulus in the environment could be harmful. In homo sapiens like us, that particular survival part of the ancient brain is called the amygdala.

Your ancient brain's amygdala fear reaction gets activated when it catches wind of any life-threatening danger. Back in the day, the amygdala's alarm was the only way we'd survive a run-in with a saber-toothed tiger. When triggered, it tells the hypothalamus to order the adrenal glands to release a stress hormone to increase your heart rate and breathing (adrenaline) and provide extra blood sugar and blood pressure to give you enough energy to respond (cortisol).

The body is fascinatingly efficient: since taking the time to think, *"EEEK, a tiger!"* in our executive functioning brain (the prefrontal cortex) would waste valuable seconds for survival, the amygdala can actually bypass the rational cerebral cortex entirely to trigger your stress response.

That's why you can feel afraid without knowing why, and why the "logical" voice in your head can tell you there's nothing to fear but your feelings can say differently. You're not crazy — it's survival science.

Since we, thankfully, live in a time when saber-toothed tiger encounters are relatively rare, the modern human's amygdala is more often triggered by fear of losing psychological things like safety, security, or acceptance instead of risk of physical harm.

In this context, the amygdala activation when you're considering changing something about your career makes sense: there are a ton of reasons to be nervous or scared about a transition because there are risks of psychological loss. You might be concerned about financial ruin, the consequences of failure, or maybe even a fear of success. (Fear of success could be feeling afraid of other people's opinions of your new path, or fear you aren't worthy of a new job and people will notice you're a fraud or an imposter.) To the amygdala, psychological harm can seem just as damaging as its physical, which is why this fear is so effective in hampering us from taking action.

Wanted to ask for a raise but got all freaked out inside your head about it? Always dreamed about running a marathon, giving a TED Talk, or moving abroad but haven't pulled the trigger yet? You've got experience with your amygdala.

Sometimes the amygdala can be incredibly helpful. When you're walking to your car alone at night, someone starts following you, and you feel adrenaline kick in to help you run away, your amygdala looked out for you. But your brain leaps into this same fear response anytime there's a perceived threat — and we logically know career change is not quite like fighting off a saber-toothed tiger. With a non-lethal threat, the survival fear activation can be maladaptive and keeping you perpetually stuck in life-draining situations.

How do we move forward if our brains are trying to convince us we will die if we make a change?

We cannot make you stop feeling fear, but we can teach you how to start a healthier relationship with your fear and stress response.

Whenever your amygdala activates and creates a fear response, it's important to remember that fear is a feeling, not a fact. Weirdly, your fears will often try to convey helpful, important information about ways you can set yourself up for success in your transition. The mindset shift around fear to ensure you make a change happen is to notice your fears, pay attention to any helpful data points they might have, and take action anyway.

> “Fear cannot paralyze a moving target.
>
> Todd Herman

Choose courageous action, not paralysis. Whenever you start to feel fears creeping in, find a tiny way to take a step and get yourself into motion.

Simple to say, trickier to implement. If you notice yourself feeling resistance, procrastination, or an unhelpful inner monologue starting up as you go through any of the materials in this book, find any incremental way to take a step forward in your knowledge. This might mean stopping reading to journal on one single reflective exercise or clarity question. It could be sending a text message to one friend, saying that you want to process a book you're reading with them. It can even look like watching a video about what it's like to work in a new industry you're curious about. The goal is progress, not perfection, and any action that's oriented towards creating a fulfilling, satisfying future is progress.

In the coming pages, you'll get lots of opportunities to test how well you can respond to your fears with courageous steps.

CLARITY QUESTIONS:

Have you ever felt fear in the past and taken action anyway? What are examples of times you've been courageous in your life before?

Do you feel resistance or fear about a possible career change? Why do you think those emotions are coming up? What is one tiny courageous step you could take to address those feelings?

CHAPTER 6

Getting Clear on What You Want

Earlier, you learned how Phase 1 involves figuring out what you truly want and defining success on your own terms. (Remember that knapsack and GPS?) It sounds so easy, yet this part of the career change journey might be the most challenging of them all. While it can feel easy to know what we don't want, it can be really hard to feel clear about what we want.

Why is confidently identifying what you want so tricky? There are two main reasons: one is environmental, and one is structural.

Let's look at the environmental factor first. By environment, we're talking about the nature and nurture you were brought up within. When you're a tiny, precious infant, the world is supposed to bend to your will. You cry and someone comes to attend to your every need: feeding you, changing you, holding you, entertaining you. If, as a baby, you couldn't always rely on adults to tend to your needs, it was *this* early in life that you might have started developing low-level anxiousness, avoidance, or mistrust in close relationships. You learned that your needs weren't always worth taking care of, which is why this introspection and unlearning work is so important for you now.

For most of the rest of your life, the people in your external environment tried to show you what THEY wanted you to want. As you grew up, you started to do things for yourself but well-meaning adults made many decisions for you: what you got to eat (or not); what you're allowed to wear to school; what gender, sexuality, or race you're "supposed" to look like.

Seemingly well-intended course-correction comments become judgments on early decisions you made:

> *"You can't get a B in chemistry. If you do, you won't go to college or ever land a job."*
>
> *"You're too young to know who you really are."*
>
> *"You don't have time to take a nap; we need to get in the car and go."*

It's likely that if you heard comments like these, you internalized them. Not by choice, but because your brain was still growing its ability to distinguish opinions from facts. You also started absorbing messages about certain traits being labeled as good or bad: it's good to be a doctor or lawyer, bad to be too loud, good to get straight As in every subject, bad to wear sneakers to work.

The world tried to talk you out of your feelings or needs when they didn't conform, so from a young age you learned to people-please. To ignore your unique needs or beliefs. To conform.

> If you are doing healing work on a personal level because you've observed some thinking biases that you don't love, like accidental preferences around gender roles, race, religion, or more, it's important to notice where some of your painful "conforming" thoughts came from. If you ever heard statements like "Oh, sweetie, we don't play with that family," or "Yes, I know he asked you to use different pronouns, but Sam is actually still a boy," you may have extra healing work ahead of you to release oppressive beliefs passed down to you through environmental conditioning.

Society taught you that in order to receive love and approval, you need to figure out what other people want from you, instead of what YOU want from you. Your opinions are inconvenient. Having your own needs gets you in trouble, especially with people who want to control your behavior early on.

So, if you're scratching your head as an adult, wondering how you were able to buy a condo and take care of two dogs but not know what you want most in your career, these environmental factors explain part of the reason.

But anytime you catch yourself saying "I don't know what I want," thanks to your environmental influences, those words probably aren't the whole truth.

Who else besides you can know what you truly, deeply want?

Other people can take guesses and offer suggestions, but it's that tiny voice in your gut that knows if their guess is right for you. And when their guess isn't right, you can feel it on a visceral level: a pit in your stomach, tension in your shoulders, a physical recoil.

So the truth is more accurately something like: *"It's become adaptive for me to ignore what I want." Or maybe, "I'm not used to being empowered to say what I want immediately or publicly."*

Like we covered in the introduction, this doesn't mean there's anything wrong with you. If this is your truth right now, there's no shame in this game. It happens to TONS of us: impulses to conform or people please at the expense of being clear about our own preferences. Almost everyone goes through a season of people pleasing in their lives because it can sometimes be adaptive and helpful. You've probably seen the advantages of people pleasing in the workplace: if you pick the right manager to compliment or agree with, you can gain favors like bonuses, raises, or insider intel. Leadership coach Nariah Broadus shared a great example of this when she was a guest on The Career Clarity Show podcast: she observed that the unifying factor among the people getting promotions at her previous job was a particularly friendly relationship with one specific leader.

But, clearly, people pleasing can also get in your way. If people pleasing is a stuck point for you, there's encouraging news: you can absolutely re-learn how to innately know what you want. It's simply a system of thinking, or a brain muscle, you can build over time.

To give a loudspeaker to your wise inner voice that may have been hushed for decades, we need to teach you new ways to listen to your deepest knowing. The best way to start to do that is by accessing the truth that lives inside the cells of your physical body.

We have different ways of listening, or "knowing" the truth of things. First, we have the cerebral and analytical way we're most familiar with. This is the "thinking" way of knowing: relying on reason, rationality, and logic to look at the day's weather forecast and determine if it's cold enough that you need to grab your North Face jacket. Thinking is the way of knowing that's easiest to articulate to others and relies on the executive function powers of your prefrontal cortex. As you recall from Chapter 5, your amygdala is a component of the brain structures referred to as the "ancient brain," the parts most deeply ingrained and central to species survival. The prefrontal cortex, on the other hand, is a much newer part of the brain in evolutionary terms. It's built outside and on top of the ancient brain, like a post-factory hardware upgrade or a fancy after-market backup camera. It's a brain part that separates us from our invertebrate brethren because it adds so much sophistication to the way we can function. The prefrontal cortex helps us with higher-level cognitive processes like planning, decision-making, problem-solving, self-control, and acting with long-term goals in mind.

But the logical prefrontal cortex, while rational and thoughtful, isn't the be-all, end-all source of knowledge. Picture this: you're walking home from a night out and turn onto a dark street. You've walked this route a hundred times before, but for some reason, this time you feel the teeny hairs on your arms start to prickle and stand up. As far as you can see, there's nobody else there, but you're picking up some other piece of information that makes it feel unsafe. (That's instinctive and immediate amygdala activation kicking in.) You grab for your keys so you have something to defend yourself with. You can try to rationalize your safety all you want, but if it doesn't feel safe, your brain can't talk you into truly being calm and chill. However, your prefrontal cortex will still try, by saying: *"You've walked this route home a hundred times before. There is no visible danger. Continue as planned."*

We can sense a truth in our feelings and intuition — a truth that our rational brain doesn't fully understand. Your logical prefrontal cortex will try to override the unexplainable feels and attempt to convince you of something else. Ever thought something that sounds like this?

"Working out is good for you. Even though you're exhausted, you'll feel better once you do it."

"It's true that you don't like that person anymore, but your families have been friends for so long that you really are obligated to go to her wedding in Omaha."

"He didn't mean to hurt my feelings with that comment about my hair in front of the whole office."

By engaging in rationalizations like these, our brains are conceding that there's a second, conflicting way of seeing these situations that they're making an argument against. The fact that you're feeling conflicting desires in the first place signals there can be multiple ways to understand a situation. Your rational prefrontal cortex, your instinctive amygdala, and your emotions all give you information to help you decide what feels truest for you.

However, this tension between different ways of "knowing" is why we learn to ignore or discard our own feelings when they're inconvenient. Your prefrontal cortex is convinced that it is the one source of all knowledge and truth, and that emotions, hormones, and intuition can all step aside.

Here's the rub: in order to find work that will truly suit you, you need to learn how to tune back into those intuitive pulls and gut feelings. Whether or not you listen to them, they're there… so learning how to start using them again shouldn't be too intimidating.

If you're not sure how to tune back into those deep-seated feelings, here's a great exercise for you called "Calibrating Your Inner GPS."

To guide yourself through this exercise, start by getting comfortable and closing your eyes. By taking the visual cortex temporarily offline, you'll be able to better tune into your other senses, including your physical sensations.

Then, think about a ridiculously happy memory. One that makes your heart leap with joy. It doesn't have to be from a time at work: your sixth birthday party at the roller rink or your wedding day works just as well as getting a rad promotion.

Let yourself bathe in that awesome memory. Visualize yourself there, in the day, in the individual moments. See what you saw, taste what you tasted, remember the moments you were laughing or smiling.

Now, ask yourself: *how did you know you were happy in that moment?*

Your logical brain might tempt you here with the thought, "I just knew," but don't let it get away with that shortcut. Sit with the weird, cerebral question for a moment. Your body gave you really clear signals to indicate your happiness. What were they?

Start with the signs that anyone else looking at you might have noticed: smiling, laughing. Think about traits that might be more unique to your particular experience of happiness: energized gesturing, relaxed posture, lots of hugs or high fives, blushing, initiating more plans, being super agreeable, asking more questions about other people, sharing more proactively about your own life, or even tears of joy. It's important for you to know your unique happiness fingerprint, because your happiness symptoms might have a different meaning to someone else.

Once you've observed several external signs of happiness, change your focus to your inner world. What did you notice happening on the inside when you're happy? Maybe you breathed easier, took deeper breaths, felt tension melting away from your shoulders, sensed warmth in your chest, felt a pulse of energy within your body, or noticed your heart rate slowing down (or speeding up!).

You may also have noticed a change in the way you were thinking. When we're getting more endorphins, serotonin, or dopamine in our bodies (the hormones that lead to feeling happiness), we often start to think different, more empowered, and optimistic thoughts. You might stop sweating the small stuff, give others the benefit of the doubt, or find a wellspring of gratitude that's easy to access when you're in a happy moment.

You might have an easier time staying in the moment and savoring the present when you're tuned into a happy state. For me, this happy-based thinking switch is so profound a change in the way I think that it's become a key signal that I might be sliding into a season of depression. Seemingly out of nowhere, everything feels like it gets hard, is never going to happen for me, leaves me feeling at the mercy of my circumstances, makes me think I'm disempowered, and seems like there's no hope or light at the end of the tunnel. These are really good warning signs that I need to get back into a regular schedule with my therapist.

Each of the emotional and mental signs of happiness you observed in this exercise is important: these are the breadcrumbs you leave yourself when you're moving toward joyful experiences. If the goal of this career discernment journey is to infuse more enjoyment, satisfaction, and fun into your work life, bring yourself back to these breadcrumbs or symptoms of happiness. As you'll be making decisions along this process, if you get stuck on knowing what you want, start with this simple question: which direction or idea makes it easier to feel happy?

Now, while we want to angle toward more joy in your work, we have to acknowledge that not every day will be purely joyful and perfect. My partner started out his career as a middle school music teacher, and for most of his life he felt like he was living his calling. He felt huge alignment, fulfillment, and had a sense of spiritual connection to the daily work. But not every day was a good day. Sometimes students were disrespectful. Sometimes parents got upset with him about what their kid did (or didn't do). Sometimes the patience he drew upon to teach hundreds of children every single day ran low. And recently, he found out a former student committed suicide, which is a tragically common experience for educators.

Pain and tragedy are part of life, part of being human, but your job itself doesn't have to be a constant source of pain. You can be in a strong fit job that allows lots of space for joy and still have very, very hard days.

The goal is to have more joyful days than hard days, and to pick a journey that you'll enjoy. That means we need to calibrate your internal GPS one more time, but this time to notice what you'd like to feel less of. This time, close your eyes and bring forward a memory of something that made you decide "never again."

Like last time, it doesn't have to be a work-related situation, but you may have several "never again" work moments that are top of mind. It could be a time that a professional relationship imploded, you were "voluntold" to do a project with someone you didn't respect, or you signed up for a professional development class you didn't want because your boss thought it was a good idea.

Now again, put yourself right back into that memory, let it be vivid, and allow those "never again" feelings to wash over you. (We primed you to hold space for the less sunny emotions in Chapter 4, so this is a good way to test how you're doing with developing that emotional awareness muscle.)

Ask yourself the same question: *how did you know it was a "no" for you in your body?*

Bypass the logical parts, because you'll always be able to rationalize why bad things happened in hindsight. But in the moment, you made the decision you did, no matter the logical reasons. So what did you feel before, during, and after that moment?

Looking at the externally observable data points, you might remember making a face, grimacing, making yourself physically smaller, crossing your arms tightly over your chest.

Turning inward, you might have noticed other sensations. Maybe you stopped breathing or felt your breaths become shorter and faster. You might have noticed your blood pressure rise or energetic tension start to fill your arms. You could have sensed a pit forming in your stomach, nausea, a desire to run away, or even a tiny voice inside you speaking up more loudly than usual and telling you to stop.

The presence of these factors is just as important as the "happy" sensations you explored before. Often, we don't feel deliriously happy at work all the time, but we tolerate and accept far more of these kinds of "never again" feelings than we realize. Take a few notes on those body signs of a "heck no" for you, in case you'll need to refer back to them along your journey to help you keep moving towards a clear "hell yes."

In addition, starting to check in with your bodily experience daily is a huge step toward finding work that will consistently feel good for you. More in-the-moment awareness allows you to enjoy every step of the journey instead of pushing yourself through hell with the hope that, once you cross the finish line at the end of the imaginary career race, things will all be different.

> "Attaining lasting happiness requires that we enjoy the journey on our way toward a destination we deem valuable. Happiness, therefore, is not about making it to the peak of the mountain, nor is it about climbing aimlessly around the mountain: happiness is the experience of climbing toward the peak.
>
> Tal Ben-Shahar

CLARITY QUESTIONS:

What are your personal happiness signs? What are the external physical signs, internal physical signs, and thought patterns that help you know you're joyful?

What are your personal "hell no" signs? What are the external physical signs, internal physical signs, and thought patterns that help you know you're making a decision that conflicts with your values?

How could you start checking in with your bodily sensations more regularly during your week?

CHAPTER 7

Dealing with Doubts Along Your Journey

As you're developing your self-awareness capabilities, you might be reflecting and noticing a fair number of happy AND unhappy emotional experiences during a given work day. When you both know that you want a change but you also see the happy moments, you might start to question whether you can trust the intuitive guidance we just spent the last chapter calibrating.

As you collect more positive and negative moments in your daily life, you might find yourself wondering, *"Is this actually that bad? Am I just ungrateful?"*

These questions are symptomatic of one of the two core thinking traps that keeps smart people like you stuck in bad jobs.

The first trap is what I call "gratitude shaming." Gratitude shaming happens when you're afraid you don't appreciate what you already have enough, so you beat yourself up and tell yourself that you don't deserve anything better.

It might sound like an inner voice saying: *"You're lucky to even have a job! What makes you think the grass is greener anywhere else?"*

You tell yourself that because you've got it pretty good but aren't appreciative enough right now, you don't deserve a job that's any better.

When you weaponize gratitude against your true feelings, it sends your brain the message that your ambition, hunger for growth, and desire to contribute on a bigger scale aren't valid. That you can't trust your feelings. That, despite your emotional reaction, you're perfectly happy, satisfied, and uninterested in anything else. Your brain begs you to be happy where you are and with what you have, at the cost of your happiness or opportunities to advance. It convinces you to minimize your craving for more challenge, appreciation, and impact.

What a weird line of logic. Let's apply this thinking trap to a different arena. Say you're eating a handful of almonds for breakfast because, on paper, it's a great nutritional decision. All those omega-3s and the plant-based protein! Except you start to notice that your stomach is upset after eating them in the morning. Nobody in their right mind would say, "You're not appreciating the nutritional value of those almonds enough. Keep eating them until you're grateful for all the vitamins and healthy fats they're giving you!" Anybody who is truly concerned about your well-being would say, "Uh, maybe you have a food allergy? You should stop eating almonds in the morning and find another way to get the nutrients you need."

You can absolutely feel both grateful for what you have (a job, something to eat for breakfast) and also crave something fundamentally different (a more fulfilling job and a breakfast that doesn't ravage your stomach). Especially when we spend more waking hours at work than we spend doing ANYTHING else between the ages of 21 and 65(ish). If you're giving so many hours of your brain, heart, and energy to something, you deserve to feel fulfilled by it.

The other fear-based thinking trap that keeps people stuck is inner character doubt. If you have this, it makes you ask: *"Am I running away, instead of sticking it out when things get tough?"*

Considering leaving your line of work and trying something new is challenging enough, but this doubt comes with a subtext that questions our deepest character: "*Have I become the kind of person who leaves, instead of stays, when things get hard? Am I a flake, a bad person, or incapable of perseverance and grit in challenging times?"*

You're right to recall that work has challenges for everyone — and there's certainly no such thing as a "perfect" job.

We all aspire to be the kind of people who lean in when there are challenges. People who run into the burning building instead of running away. Friends who show up during the hard times instead of ghosting. But it's hard to persevere when things are consistently crappy, whether in work or in life.

We need a strategy to know when it's time to run toward the challenges and stay versus when the smart thing to do is to leave.

The first thing you need to think about is whether your job, team, organization, or sector makes you feel small or like you're violating your morals.

Even though this sounds obvious, remember that we spent the last few chapters tuning back into our feelings because we can get so wrapped up in the day-to-day "doing" of our jobs that it's hard to stop and think about how we feel.

When I worked in communications consulting, I never gave myself a chance to think about how it felt to do great work for companies whose agendas I didn't agree with. I carried on, completely engrossed in the denial stage of grief, until the day my grandfather died.

When I went into that meeting with my boss, tears in my eyes, having just received the news of my grandfather's passing, and she told me I should take all the time I needed to grieve… but turned around and implied I needed to start working on a new project for her or else, I'd never felt so dehumanized. My rage opened my eyes to the violations of my moral code that had been building for years. It was not a question of my commitment of character, it was a question of hers.

If your work environment makes you feel disrespected, stupid, or unimportant in any way, trust your gut that it's time to leave.

But if you typically feel respected, valued, and motivated at work, the second thing to ask is whether you're the same person you were when you accepted this job. Sometimes you're ready to leave a job purely because you've evolved in one direction and the company or industry is evolving in a different one. Do your values, needs, and priorities align with where this role and career will take you? If not, leaving is likely the best decision for you. You can still choose to stick it out, but the longer you do, the more acutely painful the gap between your values and theirs will become.

If your intent is to be happy, you're probably not going to change what you value to suit the role, so it's a good idea to bail out instead of suppressing who you are. (If you don't believe in higher education, you probably should stop working at a university. If you're not on board with fossil fuels, you aren't going to be happy, no matter how great the job is, at an oil extraction company.)

The last thing you need to check is if you've asked for advice about your current career situation.

Usually, I'm a big believer in listening to your intuition over external guidance, but sometimes gathering different perspectives can help validate or expand your inner wisdom.

When we're tempted to run, it's often because we feel we've exhausted our internal resourcefulness. We're out of fresh water to drink in our backpack, so it's time to turn around and abandon our quest. But seeking advice from others, as vulnerable as it feels, can help us find freshwater springs that might be hiding in plain sight.

Explaining your situation aloud to someone who you trust can help you gain clarity and perspective simply from the telling. If you're noticing your listener grimace or gasp as you retell all the details about your work issue, you may get your answer.

It feels much more satisfying to leave a bad work situation if you've done everything in your power to change it. When you feel you've left no stone unturned, you can quit with confidence. You deserve to feel confident and clear about your decision to explore what's next, so ponder these points to help you figure out if you're ready to embark on a career change exploration journey.

If you're tempted to mitigate the doubts this chapter brings up by telling yourself you'll leave your current job for the "right" opportunity one day, we have one more thing to talk about.

The idea there's a "right" job out there is fundamentally flawed, and originates in perfectionistic thinking.

A working definition of perfectionism, pieced together from studies done by Gordon Flett of York University and Paul Hewitt of the University of British Columbia, is: *"...a personality trait characterized by a person's striving for flawlessness and setting high performance standards, accompanied by critical self-evaluations and concerns regarding others' evaluations."*

A perfectionist's biggest fear is being wrong or defective, so they tend to be obsessed with doing things incredibly well. This trait, like so many things we wrestle with as we grow up, can be traced to early childhood experiences or people-pleasing roots, so it's fairly common in adults. Perfectionism is often a motivating force behind high performance, so if you're ambitious or an overachiever, you may have a mean streak of perfectionistic thinking. Knowing you've been able to successfully land jobs in the past, it makes sense you'd want to find that one, perfect, "right" job before taking another leap.

But there is no single job that will completely fulfill you, meet all your socializing needs, pay you a million dollars a year, and fold your laundry for you. (Sorry.) There are actually probably quite a few jobs that could be a very strong fit for you and your 4 Pillars, but each will come with a list of pros and cons that you'll need to make strategic tradeoffs around to feel satisfied and happy. By only looking for the one right job, you'll probably miss tons of great jobs that would be a huge upgrade, feel more fulfilling, and give you plenty of space to grow.

> " Perfectionism is the belief that if we live perfect, look perfect, and act perfect, we can minimize or avoid the pain of blame, judgment, and shame. Perfectionism is addictive because when we invariably do experience shame, judgment, and blame, we often believe it's because we weren't perfect enough. So rather than questioning the faulty logic of perfectionism, we become even more entrenched in our quest to live, look, and do everything just right.
>
> Brené Brown

As you'll see in the coming steps, a necessary condition of finding great work for you is willingness to try new things, be vulnerable, and be a beginner. The openness to trying something you could mess up or not be perfect at will be the most important part of identifying the direction you want to grow in next.

When you embark on this journey, instead of asking yourself the closed-ended question of what's the "right" career for you, play with shifting your inner monologue to ask more empowering, growth-oriented and open-ended questions. They could be questions like: "*What careers might give me more room for learning and advancement? What work would be more fun for me?*

What are the different ways I could get more of the things I'm craving?"

With new questions like these, you can claim and own the upsides of perfectionism — a sharp eye for editing and improvement, a bigger picture vision for how amazing something can be, and a sense of constant iteration — as superpowers in how you approach this exploration.

> " If you don't change yourself, no career change is giong to bring you what you want.
>
> Kathy Caprino, M.A.

CLARITY QUESTIONS:

Have you ever "gratitude shamed" yourself? What are the reasons you deserve to make a move into a more fulfilling career?

Have you ever had inner character doubts? Have you taken the steps to feel comfortable that it's not you, it's the job?

Have you ever caught yourself in perfectionistic thinking? What's a mantra that could help you focus on openness, experimentation, and growth in this process?

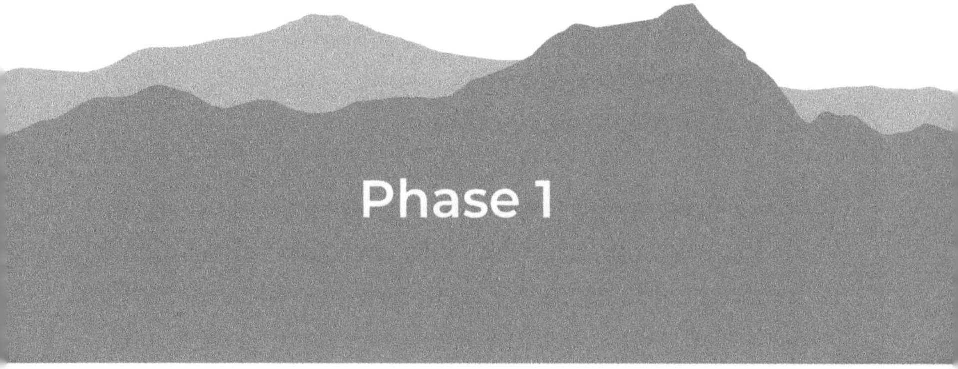

Phase 1

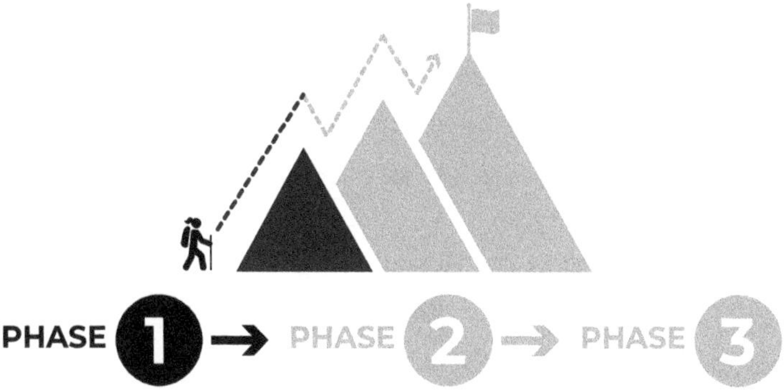

You might be picking up on something by now: learning the signs of inner knowing and clarity about what you want is different from knowing the information that gives you a sense of clarity. That's exactly where the 4 Pillars of Career Fulfillment come in during Phase 1. This framework will help you organize and process the information so you can apply your "knowing" tools to make initial decisions and generate ideas.

Now that you've calibrated those knowing skills and your mindset, you're ready to get on a first-name basis with your values and needs — understanding them as clearly and deeply as possible.

The way most people are taught to look for jobs is by starting with the marketplace: what jobs are currently available? What are people hiring for right now that you can do? Can you contort yourself to fit what they need? We're taught to only think about how to be what a job needs us to be, and that mode of thinking makes fulfillment elusive. This employer-first approach leads you away from clarity because it's rooted in your past competencies and meeting the company's needs over your own. Understanding what makes you YOU will help you differentiate between the good-looking possible roles and the great-fitting ones.

In Phase 1, you'll walk through each of the 4 Pillars of Career Fulfillment — Strengths, Magnetic Interests, Personality, and Lifestyle — to understand what they look like for you. The goal is to crystallize your most important values in each pillar so that you have a holistic evaluation of the career paths that could best fit you.

Then, you'll go through a prioritization process to separate the "nice-to-have" from the "non-negotiable" values. From there, you'll brainstorm possible career directions based on your values and priorities so you'll end Phase 1 with a short list of career options to explore and experiment with in Phase 2.

Ready? Let's grab your knapsack and prepare for this leg of your career exploration journey.

CHAPTER 8

Pillar 1

Identifying Your Strengths and Gifts

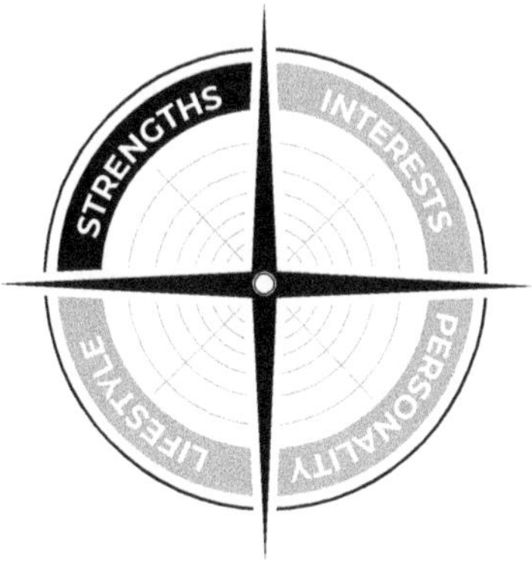

Identifying your strengths is one of the biggest factors in finding a great, fulfilling career.

If you've read even one book or article about careers, you're probably familiar with the idea of using your strengths in your job. Piles of research studies — from esteemed workplace consulting firms like Gallup to academic research powerhouses like the University of Michigan's Ross School of Business — emphasize how critical strengths are to career satisfaction. Everybody talks about that using your strengths is important, but few people take the time to define what a strength actually is and how to identify it.

Unfortunately, when we try to figure out our innermost gifts on our own, we often assume our strengths must be the professional things we're pretty good at doing. That definition isn't terribly helpful for a couple reasons.

The first reason that's a crappy way to define strengths is that almost everybody who's currently dissatisfied at work is likely good at learning new things. If I give you a brand new challenge ("Learn how to create a project plan!" "Learn how to write HTML code for this website!"), I'd bet serious money you might get excited about the challenge itself because learning is intrinsically motivating for curious, ambitious folks — even when it's learning something you may not want to do for the rest of your life. So defining your strengths as the stuff you're already good at limits you when you're motivated by getting good at new and different stuff over time.

The second reason we've got to define strengths differently is because people who are great at learning lots of different skills aren't always constantly checking in with themselves about if they enjoy using them and want to continue using them for the rest of their careers.

In his book *Excellent Sheep*, former Yale University professor William Deresiewicz described a compelling (and also concerning) conveyor belt he saw many students ending up on. As a young kiddo, you started showing promise in elementary school, and well-meaning parents, teachers, and coaches who wanted you to have access to every opportunity started expecting (and, for some of us, demanding) high grades and top performance in every subject, as well as in every extracurricular endeavor.

We developed the people-pleasing and perfectionistic tendencies discussed in Chapters 5 and 7 because of this subtle (and sometimes not-so-subtle) pressure — and our innate desire to make our parents happy. We learned to ask "how high?" when our teachers told us to jump through hoops on quizzes and papers so we could get honor roll kudos and high fives at home.

We became well-trained academic thoroughbreds, excellent at running the race of high school and college but more and more disconnected from soul-level clarity of whether we really *wanted* to run that race. We were told the only way to get a "good job" is to go to a "good school" and get "good grades," but a lot of us find the professional world isn't the fun times and cushy paychecks we were promised when we landed our first job in our twenties.

> "The system manufactures students who are smart and talented and driven, yes, but also anxious, timid, and lost... great at what they're doing but with no idea why they're doing it.
>
> William Deresiewicz, *Excellent Sheep*

This academic thoroughbred is capable of learning and doing a veritable slew of different tasks. We fall into jobs that seem interesting but don't speak to our souls. We know we can do the work, but we rarely ask ourselves if we want to do it. We know how high to jump. So we keep advancing through the ranks and end up, a decade into our careers, looking up the corporate ladder at jobs we don't want while feeling completely paralyzed by "golden handcuffs," a foreboding sense that if we tried any other career where we're happier, we'd never make as much money as we have right now.

Imagine this situation: you arrive at the office Monday morning to find a to-do list a mile high waiting in your inbox. In one of those emails, your boss gave you a brand new project that you're dreading. The project definitely doesn't light you up. It doesn't sound like something you'd be energized by or excited about. It might be something you've proven you're competent at, but this kind of project also drains you faster than streaming video zaps your cell phone battery.

But your boss says, "Listen, you know how to do it, you've done it before, and it needs to be done, so it doesn't really matter that it drains you and doesn't use your strengths. We need you to grin and bear it. Suck it up, buttercup, and please be grateful you have this job."

This hamster wheel of suck isn't the path to career clarity or workplace fulfillment.

How many times have you done a task simply because you knew you could, not because you were excited about it, and resented the hell out of it? Nothing dims your light faster or pulls you off the path to fulfillment than doing something "because you know how" instead of "because you want to."

That's why we have to define your strengths as something different from just what you can do. It's why, after helping hundreds of talented individuals who are desperate to enjoy their work more, I propose finding your unique strengths by identifying how you want to feel at work.

Weird, I know. Why aim for specific feelings to find heightened capabilities? It's because work should feel good — not like a drag or energy suck. I am certain you're a smart, talented person who could achieve anything you put your mind to. But a huge component of finding fulfilling work is becoming a champion of your joy, rather than just your abilities.

Just imagine leaving work each evening excited to work on your projects again the next day. Still having energy left to give and happily hopping over to the gym, playing with your kids for an extra half hour, getting excited about cooking something new, or investing that excess pep into fun creative projects after dinner.

Getting out of bed the next morning is no problem. You're excited to grow and learn even more, and almost feel this magnetic pull toward your projects. You experience that losing-track-of-time "flow" feeling and really feel like you're operating in the zone. That weekend anxiety about the coming workweek known as "Sunday Scaries" can become a thing of the past.

This doesn't have to be a dream. You just have to stop thinking about work as something that only uses your capabilities and instead look for ways to work using your enjoyable energizers.

Anybody who got consistently good grades knows the difference between the "capable" and "energized" operating state. You got an A in classes you disliked only because you "had" to, pulling yourself kicking and screaming through each homework assignment even though you felt drained afterwards. And despite loving your English class (or biology or calculus), you didn't get to invest tons more time or energy there because you were too busy spreading your energy across less-motivating classes.

So, for our purposes, let's define strengths as the things you can do that you enjoy doing and that give you energy.

Note that you'll often already be good at these things and get better results than your peers doing these tasks. But don't make that the chief criterion for defining your strengths. If you do, it's no longer about you. It's instead about the exact composition and diversity of your peer group. Plus, this compare-and-despair mentality can trigger your inner perfectionist and leave you in paralysis instead of searching for what's next.

My counter-culture assertion is that it's more important to lean into your energizing, exciting strengths than your existing capabilities because you can always get better at your energizing strengths (so you get more capability AND more energy). It's a lot harder to make your existing skills magically feel more energizing or inspiring for you.

I can already hear your inner hard-on-yourself voice piping up: *"If I only do things I enjoy all day and night, I'll come across as entitled and nobody will want to hire me. I'll end up on the streets, out of money, and unemployable."* In the hundreds of people I've supported, I've never seen this happen. (Permanently, anyway: some people desperately need a sabbatical to recover and rest up for the next exciting project, and can structure a way to take a break.) The point of identifying your energizers is not to only do things you enjoy 100% of the time, it's to use your joyful strengths in the majority of your work so you have leftover energy to manage other parts of work that don't light you up the same way.

So how do we even start taking a magnificent, three-dimensional creature like yourself and distilling your capabilities into a select number of energizing, enjoyable strengths?

Don't worry. It's not rocket science, although it's a nuanced awareness that will take some practice.

In Chapter 6, when we talked about calibrating your internal GPS, you started developing your self-awareness muscle. Now, you just have to use the same skillset to pay attention to the places you gain energy and enthusiasm.

When do you get lost in the flow of a project? What kinds of roles do you naturally gravitate towards when working on a team? What are the work tasks you look forward to the most? Tune into your body's signs of how you feel in specific situations at work, and find a way to track it: perhaps journaling at the end of the day, or having a note on your phone to record moments of energy and flow as you go through the workday.

As you hone and refine your internal feedback loop and start to observe moments of energy or joy in your day, don't forget to get specific. There are a few clarifying questions at the end of this chapter that can assist with this. Everyone can "solve problems" or "help people." What's more important is how *you* do it that's uniquely enjoyable and intuitive. Give yourself some guiding parameters: do I like helping individuals, groups, companies, or governments? Do I like problems that require more negotiation or more thinking? Am I magnetically drawn toward hands-on "maker" problems or more ethereal "thinker" problems?

As a caveat, when something is "easy" for you, it's tempting to believe that means it's not a true strength. In fact, it's typically the tasks that are most intuitive for us that reveal where our gifts lie. Women in particular discount their capabilities here, assuming that because they aren't the only person in the world who does something — or the skill comes easily to them — it must not be valuable. You'd be shocked how many people totally lack some of the "traditionally feminine" soft skills and gifts like empathetic listening, the ability to diffuse tense situations, or excellent coordination of moving pieces in projects.

Cindy is a great example of accidentally undervaluing one's innate gifts. Cindy was a dentist who was burned out, bored, and certain she needed to switch career paths to something new. However, as she considered several different options for Life After Dentistry, she kept feeling discouraged and fearful that her deep sensitivity and empathy were going to make it impossible to be hired anywhere because they weren't "valuable" like other hard skills. One day, as we were discussing possible options, I asked her, "What if your sensitivity to others' needs and empathetic listening are your secret superpowers? What kind of industries or environments might desperately need — and want — someone with those strengths?" Immediately, you could see a change sweep across her face. This way of seeing herself and her strengths opened up new avenues for exploration, where she could see and believe a reality where she might be paid *for* her compassion. We went on to investigate having her do project management in technical industries where empathetic communication was sometimes scarce, like engineering, and differentiate herself with this treasured, uncommon, and highly compensated compassion skillset.

If you identify as a highly sensitive person (or, for those in the know, an HSP) like Cindy, taking stock of your strengths with an external sounding board like a coach or mentor can be invaluable to help you reframe the way you see yourself, too.

At this point in the reflection process, it's natural to start wondering how you translate all this great information about your strengths into a future role. The temptation to immediately jump from strengths identification to job searching is strong because society (and most online job search tools) treats strengths like they're 100% of the fulfillment picture. Usually, we make decisions based solely on skill or capability match, at the expense of all other values. That way of thinking is exactly how you slap yourself with a fancy pair of golden handcuffs. While Strengths is the pillar that matters most to some people, if we focus only on a role that matches your strengths, it'll be one-dimensional for you.

So resist shortlisting jobs to apply to at this point, no matter how excited you are about what's to come. Remember we have three other pillars coming up: Magnetic Interests, Personality, and Lifestyle. Even if Strengths is your highest priority, it takes all four pillars to create a holistic picture of work that fits you.

CLARITY QUESTIONS:

Of all the things you CAN do, which ones are your favorites?

When do you lose track of time and find yourself completely in the flow of a project?

What types of projects do you actively seek out (whether at work or in volunteer capacities) because they bring you so much satisfaction?

What do your coworkers ask for your advice and help most on? What's easy for you?

What do you find most energizing within a typical work day?

CHAPTER 9

Pillar 2

Navigating Towards Your Magnetic Interests

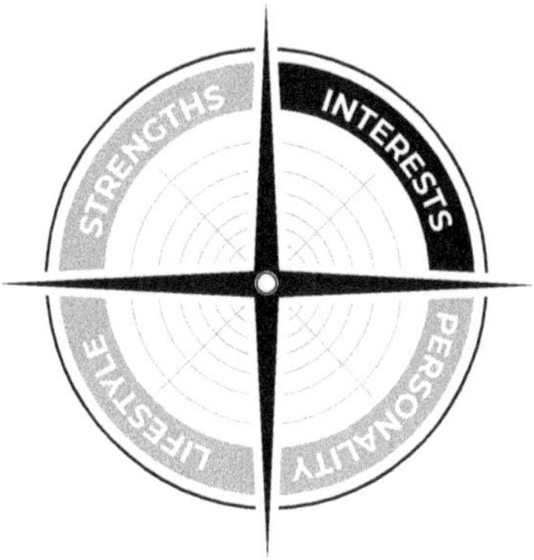

If one more person talks about the pathway to a happy career as “finding their passion,” I’m going to vomit.

It’s not because passion doesn’t exist. It’s because we’re thinking about it all wrong — and sucking the passion right out of passions.

One of the biggest concerns my clients have is that they aren’t quite passionate enough about their work.

We’ve all seen the memes about how, if you love what you do, you’ll never work a day in your life. You know the ones: those smugly smiling images of Steve Jobs and Mark Twain and other famous dead white dudes with inspirational quotes plastered in all caps across their faces.

We have this belief that you have to have passion to be excited about your work. It's something innate that you're born with and if you don't already know what it is, you're probably defective.

A pretty terrible way to feel, right? As if all hope is lost if you don't already know your passions.

If you agree that there's got to be more to life than having an innate passion, you're in good company. Georgetown computer science professor Cal Newport completely dismissed the idea in his book *So Good They Can't Ignore You*. He argues that you're not born with secret, magical passions but instead talks about passion as something you develop and grow over time: it's the product of developing skill in the work, not the impetus.

> “Compelling careers often have complex origins that reject the simple idea that all you have to do is follow your passion.
>
> Cal Newport, *So Good They Can't Ignore You*

That's why using the word "passion" makes me feel all kinds of nauseated. We pressure ourselves to already have passions, when passion is usually developed from the one-two punch of pursuing an interesting topic with sustained effort.

Plus, if you do feel passionately about something already, it can be tricky to translate that consistently into your full-time work without burning out. The places you're likely to already have passions are within your hobbies, volunteerism, or the role you play in your family — things you may not be interested in monetizing. For example, I am extremely passionate about raw cookie dough and a cappella singing. I don't define either as my passion, nor do I currently plan on turning them into some kind of paying job. Conversely, trying to monetize a passion often sucks the joy right out of it. Anybody who's worked in the nonprofit sector — and left — knows exactly what I'm talking about. Which is frustrating, after reading so many of those damn Steve Jobs memes causes us to be mad at ourselves and shame ourselves for not getting it right.

No map to career fulfillment has you stopping at "Shametown, USA" along the way.

But we still *do* want to find a way to feel engagement, excitement, and connection to our work, given that you spend a minimum of 40 hours each week for decades of your life working on it.

That's where "magnetic interests," the phrase I use to describe the second pillar in the 4 Pillars of Career Fulfillment, comes in.

Interests by themselves are the concepts that excite your curiosity and are seeds for future passion, purpose, and fulfillment. The "passion versus interest" distinction matters because passions come with tons of pressure and expectations. There's nobody on the planet who has absolutely no interests (even if you see yourself as without passions right now). When you think about your career in a less pressure-filled way, it gives you the best possible chance to find curiosities and interests that can develop into passions, like Newport argues. You can absolutely be excited, intrigued, and committed to your professional areas of interest, even if you're not "passionate" about them yet — and if you already identify as having a deep passion for your work, three cheers for you!

But we need a lens to help differentiate and prioritize between many possible interest areas. The "magnetic" wording comes from Jenny Blake, author of *Pivot*, who talks about the importance of noticing the things you can't help but keep gravitating toward in your free time over and over again. They just have a weird attraction that keeps you coming back for more.

For some folks, identifying their magnetic interests is easy. But for others, especially parents, this is the pillar you'll struggle with the most.

When you're the kind of person who loves to help others, you get really attuned to knowing what other people's interests and needs are, and start to minimize your own. This tends to happen right after you get married or if you become a caregiver of any sort. Parents, don't fear: I promise your interests include more than just watching cartoons on the couch with your kiddos. Moving your own interests to the back burner is natural as your life and role both evolve, but it also isn't your destiny to lose your identity and self-hood. You don't have to (and shouldn't!) ignore your desires for the rest of your life.

An early client of mine, Ryan, really stalled out in this part of the career fulfillment exploration. As a single parent with two young children, he felt so overwhelmed and overloaded with taking care of the kids' needs that he practically became invisible within his family. He felt beholden to his stable and boring procurement job as the only wage-earner in the house. He also knew he was profoundly bored and wasn't showing up in his most loving, present, attentive energy with his kids. Our strategy for helping him figure out a new career path he'd enjoy started with reconnecting with enjoyment, period. He started carving out one hour a week of "me time" to explore his interests: making music, reading personal development, and watching superhero movies. He started to see that this tiny act of self-care allowed him to remember what being magnetically pulled felt like, and ultimately set him on a path to completely change careers from procurement into becoming a clinical mental health counselor.

The pathway to career satisfaction requires you to reconnect with your individual, deep-seated desires. Get ready to use the "S word" to talk about your career: to find fulfilling, juicy, life-giving work, you've got to be wildly… selfish.

I promise that being a little selfish will feel great because it helps you reconnect with your deepest desires, cravings, and needs. It may even give you permission to take action on them!

To help you identify those interest areas, my mentor and gifted career coach Adrian Klaphaak has a great way to map your current curiosities. He recommends letting yourself loose inside a Barnes & Noble and seeing what sections you naturally gravitate toward. (Don't want to hit up a brick-and-mortar bookstore? You can wander down the digital aisles, checking out the podcasts you subscribe to or the downloads in your Kindle library.) Do you head directly toward resources on leading and managing teams? Or do you tend to beeline straight for books on how to become a Scrum master? Or do you plop down on the floor with a book on the best speeches of the 20th century? Take note and start making a detailed list.

For some people, a quest to remember what it feels like to be interested, engaged, and "wildly selfish" requires tapping into who they were in a different era of life. If you're struggling here, this could mean thinking about the things you got excited about pre-kids or pre-spouse. What did you do for fun as a little kid? Or, what were your favorite extracurriculars in college? Think about the things you do when nobody needs anything from you. (Not to get too life coach-y on you right now, but if you do not experience any time when nobody needs anything from you, you may want to have a chat with your partner, family, or friends about helping you reclaim even a matter of minutes each week to spend on yourself.)

Your interests can give you hints on the kinds of problems you're excited about solving, which can point you toward a department you want to work in. For example, former client Kelly worked in outside sales and business development, but had no interest in it even though she was fantastic at it. However, from looking at her bookshelf, she knew she loved personal development, professional growth, and developing deep connections with others. Those Magnetic Interests allowed us to brainstorm new industries for her to develop and leverage her Strengths, and ultimately enabled her to make a strategic pivot she was thrilled about into leadership recruiting.

Your interests can also lead you toward the sector your organization operates in — things like media, energy, consumer packaged goods, consulting, or environmental management. Take Olivia, a person who was incredibly good at analyzing and measuring her company's initiatives but completely bored by the subject matter. She knew she had a strength in analytical thinking, so we figured out that her Magnetic Interests pillar was the most out of whack with her values, and we focused in on it. At first, Olivia wasn't sure how to turn her passion for fashion and media into a real career path in the Bay Area, and worried her interests were too fluffy to make her employable. But we got curious about what might be possible if we let her be wildly selfish and take her interest seriously. By exploring integrating her interests into the sectors of her job search, she was able to find and land a dreamy role managing advertising campaigns for fashion brands at Facebook.

Let yourself be open to how your magnetic interests might intersect with future roles. It's easy to dismiss interests out of hand, especially when you realize that you're only going to the true crime and psychic medium sections of the bookstore. But what if you could integrate a tiny bit more of that into your next career move? What if you're a business analyst now but could become a forensic detective next? Or take your analysis skills to work for a consulting firm that crunches data on trends in policing to propose public policy ideas?

If you land a job you enjoy and that gives you room to deepen your interests, you're setting yourself up to be much happier and more engaged at work. Remember, you don't want to commit to one single perfect career path just yet before we've mapped all four of your pillars. But this second pillar helps you get creative — and more optimistic — about what's possible.

And if you're feeling like generating career ideas that are this creative or exciting for yourself seems impossible, hang in there and keep going for now. In Chapter 14, after you've mapped out all 4 Pillars, we'll dive more deeply into tools that can help with finding intriguing ideas.

CLARITY QUESTIONS:

What kind of materials do you already seek out for fun to learn more about? What kind of books, podcasts, and blogs do you find yourself reading?

What you did you do for fun as a little kid?

What were your favorite extracurriculars in college?

What kind of classes do you most want to take now?

Do you have a secret dream to become a subject matter expert? If so, in what area?

CHAPTER 10

Pillar 3

Finding the Right Fit for Your Personality

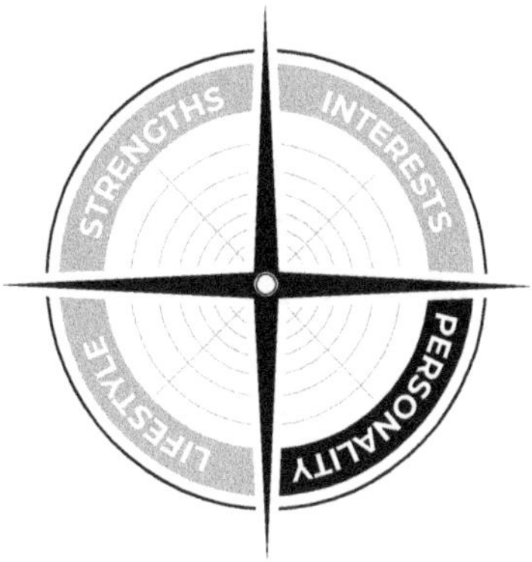

Personality fit — the third pillar of career fulfillment — is a factor that most career advice accidentally overlooks. Thought leaders tend to focus so heavily on how a job matches your strengths (and how much it pays) that they hardly talk about how important it is to find a role that fits your personality, too.

You may already know what it feels like to experience personality friction at work. This is when your job looks dreamy in its description but doesn't feel so dreamy day-to-day. You can't quite put your finger on why a "perfect on paper" job isn't feeling so perfect, but you also can't imagine staying in this role for the next five to 10 years. Even though the position uses your strengths, allows you to explore your magnetic interests, and pays well…for some reason, you still feel a weird hesitation. You wonder if there's something off about your teammates, or maybe it's the company culture? If these worries are creeping into your head, you're likely working in an environment that doesn't align with your personality.

What does it mean to have work fit your personality?

Well, your innate wiring determines a lot about your personal preferences. It determines whether you're an individual who needs lots of rules, structures, agendas, plans, and deadlines — or a person who prefers to go with the flow in their projects. It helps explain whether you get energy from collaborative, talkative environments or whether you energize better with four walls and noise-cancelling headphones.

To see the subtle importance of personality fit, let's say we're looking at someone who has a strength in technical copywriting. (This person loves to translate concepts from nerdy engineers' brains into layperson lingo.)

If we imagine personality fit doesn't matter, then it won't make a difference whether we put that person into a totally open office concept or into a workplace where everyone has a dedicated office and keeps their door closed. Their happiness and effectiveness wouldn't be affected by external noise levels, the presence of coworkers, the likelihood of being asked a quick question, or the other stimuli around them.

Neither environment is "right" or "wrong," but I bet as you were reading, you had a reflexive reaction to one of those scenarios. One of them is likely to make *you* more productive, happy, and fulfilled, and the other would probably drain you and frustrate you. These individualized preferences are a function of your personality, natural wiring, and your values.

Let's look at another example, focusing on the cultural environment created by your peers and teammates. One team is big into collaborative brainstorms, gathering input, and making decisions by consensus. The other team tends to operate more in independent productivity silos, with subject matter experts being pulled into projects sparingly and decisions being made more speedily. While you might want elements of both team cultures in your own experience, it's likely that one of these modalities appeals to your natural wiring more than the other.

One more example: company policies. Workplace A — let's call them Big Bank — is structured around lots of documented policies, clear and defined guidelines for promotions, set amounts of vacation time, written proof of all decisions, and using only legal- and IT-approved tools and resources. Workplace B — Social Media Startup — is big into adaptability, so they have social norms instead of detailed policies, unlimited vacation time, lots of opportunities to pitch for promotions, plenty of flexibility with trying new creative projects, and a willingness to beta-test innovative tools. Both companies' policies create tradeoffs, so knowing which tradeoff better fits you matters.

> “If we do not create and control our environment, our environment creates and controls us.
>
> Dr. Marshall Goldsmith

Your personal preferences map to an organization’s corporate culture, your boss’ leadership style, your team’s energy, and the interpersonal communication dynamics. Understanding your personality needs is key to evaluating each corporate ecosystem, so let’s help you get to know yourself better so you can see whether Big Bank, Social Media Startup, or some other company has an environment that will allow your personality to thrive.

Prioritizing Personality as a pillar is uncomfortable for a lot of folks because, throughout our lives, we’ve been told to act a certain way (or not). We’ve been told things like, “It’s unprofessional to speak up/swear/show up after your boss/dissent with leadership at work.”

If you belong to a minority or underrepresented group (particularly if you’re a person of color), you’ve probably been taught from a young age to shift which elements of your personality come out in different situations. Code switching, the process of identifying and displaying the “right” or expected personality traits for a certain situation, is so ingrained in your psyche that it might feel like second nature. While it might feel adaptive or needed for corporate survival, code switching usually also suppresses some of the important opinions or values that make you who you are.

If you've felt like you've needed to keep your voice quiet or inoffensive to keep your job, I'd like to propose that you've been tolerating personality fit misalignment for too long. It's well past time to look at companies who won't just tolerate you but who desperately want your unique perspective.

Seeking alignment in the personality pillar may feel both a bit radical and a bit like a homecoming for you at the same time. From the hundreds of clients I've helped, I've seen that there are workplaces out there that welcome every possible personality trait, need, or value. While it can be harder for underrepresented individuals to find abundant lists of companies where they will feel welcomed, valued, and safe, value-aligned companies are out there. Don't stop looking. Every year, companies are throwing out more of the "old (white) boys' club" social norms and systematically oppressive expectations around dress, hair, and language to foster the additional diversity and inclusivity they crave in their workforces — so these are the right standards for you to hold companies to as you search for your next career.

Just like we talked about with your magnetic interests, it's critical to be wildly selfish here. In your dream office, where do you work? How do colleagues interact with one another? What physical and cultural environment would set you up to feel delighted and satisfied each day?

> “Give yourself permission to find an environment in which you can thrive and it’s okay to be who you are. You don’t have to contort to make everybody else okay, because that doesn’t necessarily get you any further ahead and it doesn’t help those in the workplace understand the pain that’s being caused.
>
> Minda Harts

To dig deeper here, you can start exploring the nuances of your personality with assessments like Myers-Briggs Type Indicator, Enneagram, DiSC, or more. These are each fairly well known and respected tools to help you translate how you make decisions and what you prefer into the core set of values and behaviors that might help to define your needs in the workplace. In the Resources section at the end of the book, I’ve outlined a few great places to start with personality assessments, but visit GetCareerClarity.com/Bonus to get links to the most up-to-date, helpful resources.

Do you have some skepticism about personality typing tools because they aren’t always scientifically robust with peer reviewed blind studies? That wary attitude is understandable, but think about it like this: every time someone gives you a compliment, do you require them to show you 14 pieces of objectively documented evidence that has been corroborated between several other people?

Of course not. You usually hear what they say, smile, and thank them.

Or, if you're still struggling with perfectionism like in Chapter 7, you may decide you won't accept their compliment and start minimizing what they said because no amount of data points would convince you.

This exact same listen-and-resonate tactic works beautifully with personality assessments. Take the quiz, fill out the questionnaire, and see what it tells you. Maybe Myers-Briggs says you crave autonomy. Does that result resonate with you? Would you thrive in an environment where you're allowed to structure your own time? If so, write it down. If it doesn't quite feel like it fits, you're free to disregard it. Use what works and leave the rest.

From the information you're gathering about your personality needs, reflect on what your personality says about the kind of boss that will be best for you. Different bosses have vastly different personalities. As the saying goes, people don't leave a job — they leave a boss.

Understanding the type of boss who will help you feel motivated, challenged, and valued is critical and looks different for every one of us.

To identify the type of boss that will best fit you, look to commonalities between your previous favorite bosses or pull up some of the results from your personality tests for strong hints. Using the Enneagram assessment as an example, one of the core data points the instrument provides is its best guess on your biggest fear. If you fear not being appreciated, then you need a supervisor who can give you validation and approval. An unexpected tool that can be helpful here is Gary Chapman's body of work around *The Five Love Languages*, where he talks about our unique preferences in receiving affirmation and appreciation. Through the lens of love languages, there might be specific ways you crave receiving that approval, whether it's getting extra one-on-one time with them, hearing affirming words, or even getting a gift card or tiny token left on your desk. Even though the love languages were developed for romantic or family relationships, they're useful here, too.

If you've dived into the personality assessments and discovered you are an Enneagram type 1, like me, your biggest fear is being wrong. There's a reason we're called the Perfectionists — we think that if we can do everything right it makes us bulletproof, unable to be criticized, and thus worthy of love and approval. If you also tested as an Enneagram 1, you'll likely need a boss with the social sensitivity and prowess to help you grow without correcting you publicly or making you feel embarrassed in front of others.

There are nine different Enneagram types, and each one is wired a bit differently. One of the most beautiful things about exploring your personality quirks is that no set of needs, fears, or beliefs is better or worse than another. They're just different. A person who's a terrible fit manager for you might be brilliant for someone else. Start paying attention to the kinds of energies and personalities that help you flourish, and how those individuals complement your natural wiring.

Another layer of personality fit is what your personality says about your best environment to be productive and effective.

If your noise-cancelling headphones have ever failed you, you understand the importance of the physical context to your productivity and happiness. In the same way that you can do work that you're competent at but don't enjoy, you can also often find a way to push through a poor-fit environment. However, it usually comes at a cost. You may be more stressed at the end of the day and struggle to get as much done as you know you can. Knowing the right environment for you can make your happiness increase exponentially.

Your personality traits dictate the type of space that's conducive to your best work. If you took the Myers-Briggs and scored as a strong introvert (waving hello as an introverted INTJ myself!), you probably need a physical setting that has offices with doors and no spontaneous just-pop-by-my-cubicle meetings. Or maybe even a partial or full work from home policy. This is definitely true for me: while I love humans, I am infinitely more productive and happier when I work in solitude. On the other hand, if you scored as a strong extrovert, you might love a workplace that has a bullpen or open-office design with glass pop-in rooms to encourage collaboration and conversations.

If you've gone deep down the personality type rabbit hole and discovered that you're a highly sensitive person, you may need low-stimulation environments: lots of natural light and quiet. Even if you enjoy being around others, you'll need a space that has privacy so you can process how you're feeling and what's going on. You will also likely need to work with colleagues with high EQ (the IQ of emotional awareness) or in contexts that don't necessarily require a lot of emotional labor from you, as that will likely exhaust and drain you.

Physical environment is only a small part of the way that work feels each day. Beyond the relationship that you have with your boss and the type of space that's most conducive to you thriving, there's another element to personality fit that's incredibly important: shared cultural values.

For some people, a workplace that encourages you to take personal responsibility and exercise independent decision-making will be important to match up with your values and work style. For others, having a corporate culture that's constantly thinking about the sum of the parts being greater than the whole and creating opportunities for group decisions, outings, and participation might be most critical.

This can extend to team social norms: some teams are highly emotionally attuned and want to make decisions based on individuals' feelings, where other teams may decide on direction based on highly logical frameworks that aren't affected by individual circumstances. In my story from Chapter 1 about working on a team that highly valued parties, gatherings, and socializing together, the after-work boozing was a clear values mismatch with my personality. It didn't make them bad people, or make it a bad company, but it was absolutely the wrong cultural environment for me.

Don't skip over this pillar thinking you can bypass introspection because you'll know the ideal culture when you see it. Once you're clear on what values and needs make you special, you'll start to notice behaviors and decisions in others that either illustrate clear values alignment... or indicate you should probably run the other way.

For some people, personality fit will be the most important pillar — they're fine working on tasks they don't feel super passionate about as long as they're surrounded by a great boss and team. (For me, personality fit is absolutely my highest priority.) But for others, they may discover they're willing to be flexible on personality fit in order to get things they treasure even more. The key is to be as wildly selfish as you can.

CLARITY QUESTIONS:

When you take personality assessments, which descriptors resonate most? What do these traits say about the values you hold?

What kind of behaviors from a supervisor would most encourage you to perform at your best?

In your dream team, how do colleagues interact?

What physical office environment would set you up to feel delighted and fulfilled each day?

CHAPTER 11

Pillar 4

Fitting Your Career and Lifestyle Desires Together

The final pillar of career fulfillment is Lifestyle, and it's one people have a rather complicated relationship with.

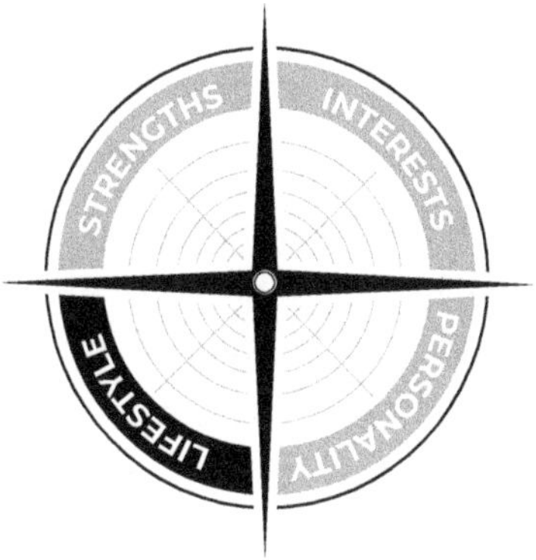

I grew up with certain beliefs about work that affected how I approached Lifestyle: the whole reason you tried so hard in school was to get a good job, and picking that perfect career was critical. After all, your job was supposed to be a defining part of who you are and how you show up in the world.

Thus, when I graduated from college, I moved to Washington, D.C. and started working at a nonprofit with a mission to change the world. While I felt deeply committed to the cause — and the role definitely used my strengths — the salary was rough. My roommate and I would sit on the floor of our apartment each weekend, bring in the newspaper, and clip coupons to save a few cents on toothpaste or orange juice. Paying for a car, insurance, or gas was out of the question, so I'd walk up the hill from the grocery store every week, no matter the weather, laden with bags. (A hard-earned lesson: always tell the cashier to double bag my soymilk.) I'd typically only see my friends when we hosted game parties or at $1.50 beer nights at the local bar. Despite not liking beer, it was the cheapest thing I could buy to fit in and be social.

Knowing I wanted to succeed as an adult, I tried to grin and bear each day of low pay and depressing work-life balance. I was lucky to have even gotten a job, and tons of bright-eyed, bushy-tailed young people would be glad to take my place, so I felt like I needed to put in a few extra hours each day and maybe work on the weekend, too.

This way of thinking was exhausting, and made every accomplishment feel hollow. But, unfortunately, it also started to pay dividends. After a year, I moved from nonprofit work into consulting, getting a fat pay raise and suddenly being surrounded by other overachievers putting in more than 40 hours a week. The new financial appreciation from work was addictive, and I kept trying to work enough to justify my new salary and opportunity. I kept striving for "enough:" to be a good enough employee, to work hard enough, and to find a way to make the money be enough. I'd liked my job well enough when I started, but after the months and years of overwork went on, I started to resent the work. It was a paradox: everyone at the company seemed to complain about being so busy and working too much, but they wouldn't stop. They were proud to be in-demand in their professional lives, even if it was making their personal lives miserable.

Then, I started to notice something weird: not everyone in D.C. felt completely miserable at work.

One warm Saturday morning, my best friend invited me to meet some of her breakfast club girlfriends. This tight-knit group of women had known each other for years and would cook each other breakfast once or twice a month so they could catch up over coffee and eggs. While the breakfast club group had been meeting for a long time, they were always welcoming new transplants like me into the fold to help make D.C. feel more like home. Our first conversations struck me, because while everyone was so warm and interested in one another's lives, nobody talked about their jobs. It might have been the very first brunch I ever left where I didn't know what most people did for work. These people chose to think about work and its role in their lives very differently.

Then, a different friend introduced me to his hometown friends. They all went way back, having been neighbors and knowing each other's parents since they were toddlers. When I'd hang out with these guys for a backyard barbecue, nobody was looking at their watches because they'd double-booked with another work happy hour. Nobody was sitting on the couch in the corner answering work emails on their phone for hours.

There was something different about each of these people. Instead of asking what you did, they'd ask what your favorite TV show was, what you were up to that weekend, or what you were reading. Instead of complaining about their bosses, they would debate which grocery store had the most delicious produce.

They, to be blunt, didn't care that much about work.

It wasn't that they didn't care about work at all. But, for them, work played a very specific, defined, and limited role in their lives. Instead of life revolving around work, they created rich, holistic lives full of rest, deep connection with friends, and full presence with family members in addition to work.

They had hobbies. They had time to go grocery shopping and cook, even when parenting small children. Their romantic relationships seemed stronger and more collaborative than the ones of their workaholic peers like me.

This small but mighty cohort of individuals didn't care whether the company I worked for was prestigious or world-renowned. They cared whether I was sleeping at night, or creating boundaries that allowed me to enjoy life outside of work.

These people cared about my life as a whole. They wanted me to be happy — and even assumed I had a life outside of work! (I certainly wanted one, but couldn't ignore the notifications on my email app that never stopped popping up.)

One day after another wonderful girls' breakfast get-together, I was heading home and realized that I desperately wanted the peace and joy they all looked like they had. I was done saying that I wished I could be more balanced. For the first time, I wanted to take action to care less about my work and more about a joyful, fulfilling life. It was hitting me that the consequence of choosing to be a low-key workaholic and make work my priority was the rest of my life becoming wildly out of whack with my values.

The easiest way to create a fulfilled, beautiful life is deciding on the life you want, and brainstorming how career can fit into it.

Jill Ozovek, workplace consultant and career coach at The Career Passport, coined a brilliant phrase to describe this new way of thinking: the "good enough" job.

The mindset that allows you to find a "good enough" job means that you won't keep hustling to get into the C-Suite and earn your corner office by 42 and *then* start living your life. It means that you won't keep striving to hit traditional career milestones only to realize you don't know your spouse or kids anymore. It means you won't accidentally let your health go and find yourself in the hospital for stress-related cardiac issues, and start cultivating hobbies besides numbing out with wine, over-exercising, or streaming video binges.

If you invest all your energy and time into climbing the corporate ladder, what happens to the rest of your life when you get to the top? Is there ever really a top where you can stop striving and start living?

Society pressures us into believing we have to be promoted every other year and "complain" about overwork (and how indispensable we are) like it's a badge of honor. But the data consistently shows that, at the end of our lives, nobody on their deathbed regrets that they didn't work more. They regret not spending more time with loved ones. They regret not having more life in their lives.

Many of my clients experience a huge shift when they start thinking this way. While they want to enjoy their work, they ultimately want to work to live — not live to work.

Because of that tradeoff, they're fine with releasing their workaholic tendencies and working a decent job that doesn't get in the way of their happiness so they can live the kind of life they want outside of work.

This "life fulfillment first" mode of thinking takes all the pressure off your job to be your identity, your future, your sole source of fulfillment, and your security. (And, remember: pressured-filled thinking is a classic symptom of perfectionism running amok with your ambitions.)

To put the last pillar in place, we have to define the kind of fulfilling life you want to have outside of work — and how you want work to enable you to live your life.

Your version of a beautiful life and lifestyle is primarily tied to making choices about your values. Here are a few examples of that in action.

Maybe you're a mom who loves spending time with your kiddos. Your beautiful lifestyle might involve being able to work from home without asking for permission. That way, you can honor your value of being present with them when they get home from school while still honoring your commitment to your work. (And you can feel absolutely no guilt about working from home if someone gets sick and needs a little extra attention from momma.)

Or maybe you're a competitive marathoner. You need to work, but want to keep training because you're getting closer and closer to breaking personal records in each race. Fitting in your runs after work sucks because either (1) it's too hot; (2) it's too cold; (3) it's too dark; (4) you're too drained; (5) you want to go have a green smoothie with friends instead; or (6) you had to work late and now your whole schedule is thrown off. So the way you can honor your values (and do your training runs in the morning without getting up at 3:30 a.m.) is by working at a company with flexible hours. Maybe they have core hours where you have to be in the office between 11 and 3, or maybe they're willing to shift your workday to start at 10 a.m. instead of at 9.

Or maybe, like one of my clients, you have a child with a disability. That means the number one most important way a job can match with the fulfilling lifestyle you want is if it pays well and gives you gold-star health insurance so you can cover any surgery or alternative therapy modality your darling needs. And it's even better if they give you oodles of paid time off so you're able to take them to their appointments and stay with them in the hospital without worrying about how much time is left in your vacation time bank. We found a job that fit these exact criteria for her, but the only reason we found it was because she was super clear on what mattered most.

If any of those scenarios sound like you — or helped you immediately crystallize your own values — it's likely that lifestyle is the most important of the 4 Pillars for you. That means you'll prioritize it highest when you're searching for your next job. Instead of worrying so much about your exact job title, you'll focus on identifying companies with evidence of benefits and flexibility that fit your values.

Don't hold back in your dreaming. Let yourself be wildly selfish. (Noticing a theme in these 4 Pillars chapters?) Whether you want to buy a vacation home on the Outer Banks to host family reunions every year, take a six-month sabbatical, or start a nonprofit foundation, tie your dream to your values.

> “Dreaming, after all, is a form of planning.
>
> Gloria Steinem

Remember Ron, who you met in the Introduction? He wanted to get a six-figure role — and needed that job to be in the city where his wife had just secured tenure as a university professor. Moving cities and increasing pay at the same time is challenging but doable; however, Ron had another dream, too. He wanted his work to give him extra paternity leave, as he and his wife were expecting their first baby. Since he got crystal clear on what he valued most, he was able to successfully negotiate a bonus six weeks of paternity leave into his contract at his new six-figure job.

Maybe your inspiration can come from Flora, a marketing executive relocating to Colorado so she could spend more time in nature. She searched high and low for a senior communications job in the Denver area with more work-life balance. Her ideal option came in an unexpected but amazing offer package: work four days a week in marketing consulting for the company, and get Fridays off every single week. She accepted the role and spent her perpetual three-day weekend free time hiking and skiing in the beautiful Rocky Mountains.

There are companies out there that offer more perks than you can even imagine, whether it's a completely remote distributed workforce that pays you to fly to Thailand for company meetings or an organization that cares more about outcomes than hours and lets you work whenever you want. There are companies that give you extended, fully paid maternity leave and ones that will foot the bill for your entire graduate degree. I've even worked at a company with Dog Fridays, and everyone brought their pooches to the office for slobbery snuggles once a week.

When you give yourself permission to dream or to be honest about what you truly want, you'll start to figure out how you can actually create it.

And if you make the courageous choice to pursue work that has a huge return on investment for your happiness and energy, you'll usually be able to create the rich, nourishing, aligned life you want without having to focus on riches.

Isn't that what we all ultimately want anyway?

Let yourself paint the picture of your ideal scenario, even if it seems outlandish or impossible right now. The clearer you are about your priorities and non-negotiable values, the easier it will be to find them.

CLARITY QUESTIONS:

If you could create work-life integration beyond your wildest dreams, what would that look like?

What does having a rich and thriving personal life mean to you?

How many hours a week do you want to be working? How do you want work to fit into the rest of your life?

If you have a partner or spouse, what would you love your ideal integrated work-life balance scenario to look like? (And, don't forget to ask them directly and loop them into the dreaming process!)

CHAPTER 12

The Money Versus Fulfillment Paradox

We can't talk about having a rich life without dissecting one of the biggest hurdles between people and careers they'll love: money.

There's a common concern that income and joy are opposite forces on a paradoxical career spectrum, with "money" at one end, "happiness" at the other. If you make good money, you don't get much happiness. If you optimize for joy, you have to live paycheck-to-paycheck for the rest of your life. And if you shoot for something in the middle, you get a little of each but aren't really satisfied with either.

If you're a relentless optimist like me, this feels like a dire diagnosis.

This belief is pervasive because most of us can point to someone who is making a giant paycheck and who is downtrodden, terrified to make a change, or hopelessly resolved that their career path "is what it is."

Several years ago, I was on the phone with a potential coaching client who told me he had so much left to give and desperately wanted to make a bigger impact with his work, but also needed to be making more money.

I asked how much he was making right now.

He paused, then asked, "Before bonus, or after?"

Turns out, he was making $240,000 a year in base compensation, and was reaching nearly $300,000 with his annual bonus.

So, I pushed him. I said: "If making more money is your biggest value, it may limit the way you evaluate career moves to make an impact. Desiring more money without a clear mission for the money makes us all look at opportunities through a very narrow lens. Are you willing to consider taking a pay cut if it would increase your impact?"

He said "maybe" on the phone that day, but I haven't heard from him since. We never got to start looking at all the possible ways he could optimize his career for happiness, and which ones would best fit his financial goals.

After working with hundreds of clients, here's what I've seen is the truth to the paradox: if you pursue money as your chief value, you usually trade off a certain amount of happiness to get it. But if you pursue happiness, you can usually find a way to make the money work, too.

But no matter whether your salary is closer to $30,000 or $300,000, understanding how to optimize for a career that's both soulful and lucrative can be tricky. Financial needs are often tied to feelings of real fear and insecurity about your paycheck: how big it is, how often you get it, and what you can afford.

Money often seems like a natural vehicle to live in alignment with your values. With more money, you should be able to buy more balance because you can hire help. You ought to be able to buy more happiness because it's easier to drop cash on plane tickets to trendy tropical locales or expensive hobbies. You could buy more impact if you charitably contribute your extra income. Or even buy more freedom because you can have a fully funded, ahem, "fuck off fund" so you can walk away from your current employer and take a break anytime you want to.

But chasing higher compensation as the only means to get these ends is incredibly limiting.

Money can help facilitate some joy, but it won't create a joyful, fulfilling life by itself. For many folks, they want a certain amount of money because they equate it to certain investments, a specific job title, or a house in a particular neighborhood. But investments, titles, or property aren't necessarily valuable in and of themselves. They're valuable because of what they help us to feel:

investments help us feel safety or freedom, titles help us feel proud and accomplished, and a home you love can help you feel secure or peaceful. Consider this: if you feel you have security, community, and joyfulness while making $30,000 a year, you might actually feel pretty contented. But if making $30K gets in the way of feeling safe and secure, you'll probably start checking out job postings immediately.

Pursuing money with the belief that dollar bills by themselves will lead you to tons more happiness doesn't play out in the data. In the 1970s, economist Richard Easterlin did a study of self-reported happiness levels in different income brackets. His findings showed that levels of happiness remain relatively stable no matter what amount of money you're making. While more recent studies show a wee bit more correlation between income and happiness, marginal happiness doesn't increase much once you're making over $70,000 per year in salary, adjusted for cost of living in your market. If that's true, a desire to make more money to get to more happiness is flawed because when we finally get more money, our happiness isn't going to change significantly. The term from psychology about how positive changes in our lives don't typically cause lasting changes in happiness is: "hedonic treadmill." Imagine it like a capitalistic hamster wheel.

Behavioral economics research also says there's a big difference between how we imagine we'd spend extra money and how we actually do. The "wealth effect" is an economic trend where, when you have more money, you typically spend more, so savings rates don't usually increase. The data says that we usually take it for granted that our new income is going to be our new normal, and increase our purchasing accordingly. Instead of saving up a freedom fund, trying to create financial independence, or starting that nonprofit, we usually end up buying a more expensive home, getting a nicer car, or buying more expensive jeans.

Do these purchases increase our happiness? Sometimes, though thanks to the hedonic treadmill, it doesn't usually last.

Do these expenses limit our ability to do other things and pursue the rest of our values? 100%.

We want more money because it seems like the surest pathway to freedom. But instead of feeling free when we make more, we sometimes slip on an upgraded pair of golden handcuffs. Our decisions about spending can become the subconscious chains that bind. Perhaps The Notorious B.I.G. was right: mo money *can* mean mo problems

We believe we can't quit our soul-sucking but high-paying jobs because we need to pay for our new gym membership to help us burn off stress from work, to afford the top therapist to help us process our feelings about work, to order the lunches (and dinners) we eat at our desks because we're working so much, to afford the yoga retreat in Fiji to regain our zen after the toxic treatment we're receiving at work... you get the idea.

And when we think about how chasing money affects our lives over time, it can look bleak. I can't tell you the number of individuals I've worked with who feel like they have to make more to give their (current or future) kids a certain life, but end up working or traveling so much that they only see their kiddos on the weekend. They spend so much time away that they don't actually know their kids. Or, their children start acting out at school because they want more attention than their parents can give them because their parents are too busy trying to buy them a great life. Do you want your kids to watch you on the hedonic treadmill, trading off so many other important values just so you can watch your bank account balance rise?

When you treat money like it's the end game instead of an instrument, it can start to run — and ruin — your life.

My most successful clients don't hold money as their highest priority value. They value something else — be it balance, freedom, or contribution — more than they value money. Money is important for them because it's a tool to help create the life they want.

Let's talk about creating a plan for the life that you truly want, treating money like a tool to make it happen. This means we're going to be crystal clear on how money serves your values so you feel the way you want to feel in your life, instead of always feeling like you don't have enough.

You need to give your money a job. When you are crystal clear on what money is doing for you and where it's going, you can feel more in control and strategic about your career decisions. For some of my clients, money plans helped empower them to rest. I've had several clients quit their jobs and take a sabbatical after we mapped out their financial runway. One worked on passion projects and creating her jewelry line. Another is starting her own motivational speaking business. And other folks are taking time for detoxification and "active recovery" to refresh before jumping into their next jobs. Everyone valued taking a break, and, once they saw they had the financial safety net in place to make it happen, they went for it.

Figuring out your financial needs starts with knowing those endgame core values. Ask yourself what your current and past decisions indicate you value: do you prioritize using money to help with adventures and travels because you value options, or to have a year's worth of expenses saved up as an emergency fund because you value security? Neither value is better or worse, and you can create a plan to help yourself honor those prioritized values with your spending decisions. If you value creating a nonprofit to help families with high-needs children, budget that into your values, too. And if you anticipate changing needs, like if you're planning to have kids in the next few years and want a fund set aside for cribs, carseats, and maybe in vitro, plug that into your money plan, too.

After you've started to map out what values you want money to help you feel and honor, you need to define "enough" so you know what it takes to feel those values in your daily life.

> "Enough is a decision, not an amount.
>
> Alison Faulkner

You shouldn't limit yourself and only earn up to your "enough" line — far from it! But you've got to know what amount of money it will take you to achieve your financial goals to make smart career decisions. If you don't know what the goal is, you'll constantly be running after higher paychecks at the expense of everything else important in your life. Pursuing money endlessly for the sake of being able to dive into a bottomless bathtub of gold coins is an easy way to accidentally prioritize earning over your other values and leave you feeling totally depleted and depressed.

If you feel like you can't commit to a number in savings that would be enough because you never know what medical emergency or family crisis could be around the corner, you'll constantly be a slave to your income. When interviewing financial expert Grace Pomroy about how much you put into an emergency fund, she shared this story with me:

"My husband was injured in a serious car accident, one of the worst things I could picture happening to the person I love. Suddenly we are trying to figure out medical bills and what it means to have him out of work for a few months. The situation taught me that it is important to be prepared, but community is one of the most important things you can have. Others stepped in to fill the gaps for us financially, emotionally, with meals — community support is often what gets you through the worst of times."

The last step in understanding your current financial reality is illustrating the gap between where you are and where "enough" is. Knowing where your money is going can help you understand where you want your money to go. Once you've defined your financial goals, sometimes they are a lot closer than you think.

And sometimes, you have big ol' ambitions in your plan that are going to require you to earn more money. If you can align the things that you love doing with things that have a high market value, you can find ways to combine your strengths, magnetic interests, personality, and lifestyle into a profitable profession. You'll feel like a magician by making money and happy grow in the same direction, and proving all the stuck, grumpy people around you wrong.

If your pillars align with any of these higher salary drivers, you can create a strategy to move the needle on both joy and pay at the same time in your career change:

Increase the organization's revenue: The more you're responsible for directly bringing money into the company, the more likely you'll be compensated in kind. This could be in a sales or new business role, where you may or may not get a base salary supplemented by commission. It could look like partnership development with other businesses. It could also involve entering a new market or releasing a new product that performs well in the marketplace. It might be doing digital demand generation and optimizing ad buys or making sales funnels more efficient. In the nonprofit world, revenue-driving jobs are usually in the "development" (a.k.a. fundraising) world, working with high-dollar donors or occasionally writing big-figure grant proposals. If you bring in the dollar bills, the organization will typically reward you handsomely. If this kind of work sounds like a fun challenge for you, lean into it!

Develop niche, specialized expertise: If you have a skill or knowledge that's hard to come by, you can charge employers a premium for it. This is why lawyers, engineers, and doctors typically make bank — but developing valuable subject matter expertise is a tactic available to all of us. Rarity breeds value for the right organizations, so strategize about how to position your current expertise, or think about how to develop an uncommon specialty. I think of the Pilates teacher I had back in Washington, D.C., who was world-famous for creating a Pilates specialization for individuals with multiple sclerosis. She not only started her own studio to specialize in this work, but has been flown all over the world as a featured guest expert to talk about her approach. This is why social worker Brené Brown has had such a lucrative path in an otherwise fairly low-paying field: expertise and publicity for addressing tricky issues related to shame and vulnerability. Whether you add an academic degree or a certification — or nerd out on your own time and become a de facto expert — there are lots of possible ways to add valuable specializations to your skillset.

Increase responsibility: The greater the number of people and projects you take ownership of and responsibility for, the larger the compensation you'll likely bring home. The higher the percentage of a company's total profit-and-loss that you're in charge of managing, the larger your slice of the pie. So, if you want to try a typically lower-paying industry like education, being a classroom teacher is likely to be paid less than if you're in administration (managing more bodies). And working in administration for one school usually makes less than being the whole district superintendent. As another example, I once worked at a consulting company that prioritized promotions based on the total amount of company revenue that tracked back into your department. An easy way to set yourself up for growth here is to keep track of how many projects, clients, dollars, or people you're in charge of on a daily basis to help prove the worth of your strengths to your future employer. Even right now, you can ask for stretchy opportunities to manage more than what's in your current gig and increase your market value.

Increase profitability: In contrast to directly increasing revenue, this kind of role might be in accounting, auditing, or business analysis, where you look through the company's books and find ways to cut expenses, change vendor contracts, lock in advantageous pricing, or re-allocate resources. If you have a natural knack for process improvement, this can be a great place for you to thrive. You can also contribute to increases in efficiency and profitability from almost anywhere within an organization if you search hard enough. Look at what the biggest costs are in your department and compare those to the "value" drivers for your customers to see if there might be upside left on the table. If you love analysis, process improvement, and optimization, this is a great idea to try out.

Take on a significant amount of travel: A number of friends have accepted roles where they lived abroad for periods of time or do the Monday-morning-to-Thursday-night consultant airport commute. Sometimes this kind of work doesn't actually increase your paycheck, but it decreases your living expenses pretty significantly because all kinds of consumption costs are billable to your employer or client. If you're living out of a hotel four days a week, it may not change your rent at home, but all your meals on the road ought to be covered, thus saving you money. Plus, you can visit incredible places and often extend your trips to include some tourist days! Former coworkers of mine in the communications consulting industry commuted to or lived in Canada, Great Britain, the United Arab Emirates, Indonesia, Russia, Brazil, and more.

Increase your availability: Your compensation can increase if you're needed for hours beyond the typical Monday-to-Friday, 9-to-5. Sometimes this is directly accomplished with overtime pay if you're a non-exempt employee. Sometimes this is accomplished with spot bonuses and comp days if you're an exempt employee. But sometimes folks know that their jobs will ask for hours above and beyond traditional expectations and will build that "thank you" pay into their salary. (This is one reason why consultant pay tends to be fairly high: they hit the profitability trifecta of specialized knowledge, more travel, and more availability.) If you accept a job where you're on call for emergencies or client issues, you'd better negotiate some extra pay for potentially sacrificing personal time at unexpected moments. And remember that this is only worth going after if it's in alignment with your lifestyle values. If your ideal lifestyle from Chapter 11 involves steady, predictable hours, this one may not be a fit for you.

Increase your inconvenience: You can increase your pay by increasing the amount of inconvenience you're willing to take on. Spoiler alert: this path to more money usually sucks, unless the type of inconvenience lines up beautifully with your values in some way, like you're a night owl and totally love taking the graveyard shift or want to be a professional baker. Unlike availability (where you're asking for more pay because you may have to work at unplanned or unexpected times), inconvenience is usually planned and expected. You're the one who's working on Thanksgiving or the one who has a regularly scheduled shift on Saturdays. Increase your inconvenience at your own risk. I've seen this work well for parents: one spouse works regular hours and one works "inconvenient" hours so they always have someone home with the kids. I've also seen this work well when one parent has partial custody and works inconvenient hours on their time away from the kiddo so they can spend all their off time with the little one.

Increase your exposure to risk: I used to be obsessed with the Discovery Channel show Deadliest Catch. You know, the one where salty fishermen (or, crabbermen?) go out into the Bering Sea to set traps for valuable deep sea crabs. The reason there's a whole TV show about this industry is because you have to be wild to work in it: exposure to extreme weather, freezing temperatures, and legitimate risk to life and limb. The only reason I can imagine folks do this work (beyond being adrenaline junkies) is that it pays you handsomely for all the risk you've been exposed to if you bring in a good haul. Beyond options in working for someone else, exposure to risk is how entrepreneurs make bank. Going out on your own is gutsy, but depending on how you structure your offering, you can have huge potential earnings if you find a great intersection of product-market fit. However, there are plenty of reasons why not everyone goes out as an entrepreneur: risk tolerance, needed security, and lacking in the time, resources, commitment, or mentorship to set themselves up for success. Bring it back to your values and how high your risk tolerance is before moving forward on this one!

Between these eight paths, there may be at least a couple that intrigue you and seem doable. Pick the best option for you and you could set yourself up for higher earning potential in a career path that fundamentally aligns with your values.

As you complete your future career path brainstorm and move into Phase 2, it's natural to be concerned about the financial viability of your ideas. You think, *"Can I *really* make enough money doing something I enjoy?"* Every time one of these viability fears pops up, you have a choice: do I treat this like a roadblock or a speedbump? If you treat it like a roadblock when there's a possibility it could just be a speedbump, you artificially limit your problem-solving potential and give yourself a reason to give up. (You also set yourself up for regrets and the "what if" monster to chase you around for years to come.) If you treat it like a speedbump, it will appear like something you can creatively navigate around to keep moving forward toward your dreams. You'll be innovative and resourceful as you come up with workaround ideas. The mindset you choose as you encounter each new piece of information dramatically affects the possibilities you can create for yourself. Remember: the economy does not usually reward folks with higher pay based on seniority or likability alone. If making more money is a critical part of your dream, there's usually a lot you can control to make it happen.

A great example of someone who navigated creatively around financial speedbumps is Eric Alston, an economics and law professor at the Leeds School of Business at the University of Colorado Boulder and featured interviewee on The Career Clarity Show podcast. Eric got a master's degree in economics to qualify for the policy jobs that excited him. The problem was that he needed a terminal degree in the field to advance, and he had no interest in doing the years of research required for a PhD in economics. So, instead, he started looking at ways to get around that speedbump and keep doing the work he wanted to do. He discovered that any terminal degree in a related field would let him do the work he wanted to do, so he started exploring degree programs that sounded more appealing. Surprisingly enough, he landed on law school.

Law school is typically an incredibly pricey endeavor, leaving graduates with hundreds of thousands of dollars in student loan debt upon graduation. But Eric had a strong hypothesis about the work he wanted to do that made investing in this degree worth it. He decided to think creatively about how to get around the prohibitive costs of school. What was his solution? Eric chose to go to the law school that gave him the most aid money instead of the law school with the best or most selective reputation. By treating the financial burden of graduate school as a problem to be solved instead of an insurmountable obstacle, he's now doing work that he loves without feeling the oppressive student loan debt dooming him to a lackluster life as a partner-track attorney in a faceless law firm. It's all about mindset and making choices that create options instead of take them away.

CLARITY QUESTIONS:

What do you want your paychecks to allow you to do? What does your target lifestyle cost?

When do you have "enough"? What factors could affect that?

What would you do if someone gave you an extra $15,000 tomorrow?

CHAPTER 13

Prioritizing Your Most Critical Values

After mapping out your 4 Pillars of Career Fulfillment, you might find yourself thinking, *"Well, this is all great information and insight, but now what?"*

If we return to our hiking metaphor, you've spent a lot of time thus far evaluating the landscape, learning about the terrain, and getting the highest-rated hiking boots. You're probably itching to head out into the wild, but before you take your first step you need to decide what direction to walk. Or, at least have an idea about the mountain you'd most like to climb.

When people think about what's holding them back from finding a fabulous fit career, it often comes down to "good ideas."

You may feel like you don't have any good ideas, or you've had way too many ideas over the years: chief of staff, senior product manager, human resources business partner, social worker, entrepreneur… the list might go on. The underlying problem is typically that you don't know, out of all the career possibilities and paths out there, which ones to take action on and which ones are better left as dreams. If you don't have a system for generating strong-fit ideas, testing them effectively, and making your transition, all the ideas in the world won't help. In the same way we can't frost a cake that hasn't been baked, we have to create a unifying, strategic vision about the ideal career path for you before we decide which ideas to make reality and start rebranding your whole resume.

Your next step in creating a compelling career vision for generating great ideas is to review your reflections and insights and do some serious prioritizing. We can't hike up every single route on Mount Fulfillment at once, and we certainly can't have you carrying a backpack with hundreds of pounds of gear, so it's time to create your personalized criteria for assessing best-fit possible directions.

The first thing you're going to do is prioritize within your pillars: what are the most important, non-negotiable parts inside each pillar? Write down the top two to five things you need to feel satisfied in your Strengths, Magnetic Interests, Personality, and Lifestyle pillars.

Let's say that in your Strengths pillar, there's a hefty list of activities that make you come alive. You want to run brainstorms, develop strategic plans, do process improvement, write, edit, do public speaking, manage projects, and do media buying. While getting to do every single one of these items would be great, it will be tricky to identify a role that lets you do all of them. Therefore, you have to prioritize which of these strengths would be the very most fun and energizing and challenging for you to lean into next.

For some people, this is going to be a challenge because making prioritization decisions is almost physically painful for you. You'd rather cut off your arm than take a possible option off the table. (If you took the Enneagram personality assessment we talked about in Chapter 10 and discovered you're a Type 7, this is you!) The challenge of wanting to prioritize everything is that, as they say in the graphic design world, "If everything is bold, nothing is bold." When everything is a priority, nothing is a true priority. And if everything's a priority, when faced with competing options, you won't be able to make a decision on what you should trade away versus what you should keep.

> There are no solutions, only tradeoffs.
>
> Thomas Sowell

Choosing the things you're happy to trade off in order to get the things you really want is critical to improving your work situation. Otherwise, you'll end up constantly swirling from job to job without making consistent upgrades. To train your brain on how to make strategic tradeoffs, start with little this-versus-that binary prioritization decisions inside one pillar, like this example for Lifestyle: *"If I could either get a shorter commute or better health insurance, which one would be more important to me?"*

Another temptation is to try to generalize out your values so they're contained within a handful of broad categories, like saying you want work where you help people, where the work is meaningful, and where it's challenging. Of course you do. Everyone does! These superlatives don't help you unless you're willing to define what they mean for you. Challenge yourself to get more granular and define exactly what meaningful work is for you. One person's meaningful can be "working with businesses to make their processes more efficient so they can scale further and serve more people," while another person's meaningful might be "working one-on-one with individuals to process their grief and provide a safe space for them to practice tools to become more assertive and set boundaries."

Once you've come up with the top non-negotiable traits in each of your pillars separately, the second step is to prioritize between your pillars. This isn't because you really only get to satisfy one pillar — ideally, you're satisfied on all four pillars in your next role — it's because trying to look for 20 different traits all at once is harder than looking for the top four to five highest priority traits in your top priority pillar, and then layering on the next four to five traits in the next pillar that matters most to you.

For me, I prioritize the Personality pillar the highest, then Lifestyle, Strengths, and Magnetic Interests. If I plop myself down in an environment that doesn't suit me, it doesn't matter if I get to use my strengths every single day and work on problems that thrill me... I won't be happy for long.

Between your 4 Pillars, which one is the *the* most important for you right now?

Paying attention to the "right now" is important because, over time, it's natural for priorities to shift. Are you earlier in your career, have low overhead costs, and up for taking on more risk? Working in alignment with your Magnetic Interests might be the most exciting path for you. Are you a newlywed who's tired of coming home and complaining about how bored you are at work? Strengths might be the most important one for you in this season. Are you a single mom with multiple littles? Lifestyle is probably going to be huge for you right now.

It isn't that the other pillars aren't important, but rather that we know which one to lead with when we start brainstorming.

Most career advice says now you'd go to online job boards, search for key terms, and then apply, as if all values, priorities, personalities, and definitions of success are the same. There's no consideration of your uniqueness, priorities, or how one title might mean a dramatically different role depending on the company, industry, or size. From working with hundreds of career changers, I know the most effective job search strategy is one that adjusts and adapts based on which pillar's most important to you. We'll talk about that adaptation more in Phases 2 and 3, too, but your pillar priority will inform the way you brainstorm and create ideas in the next chapter as you translate your values into possible paths.

CLARITY QUESTIONS:

What are your top two to five prioritized needs within each of your 4 Pillars: Strengths, Magnetic Interests, Personality, and Lifestyle?

What is the highest priority pillar for you right now?

What's your lowest priority pillar right now?

CHAPTER 14

Generating Directionally Correct Career Ideas

At this point in your clarity-seeking trek, you're staring at the short list of things you need in your next job. You've pulled out your trusty career discovery map, and have started to highlight a few areas you want to make sure to explore. Maybe your heart's started beating a little faster with anxious anticipation. Or maybe it starts beating slower, feeling mopey and hopeless, and you're thinking: *"How could I possibly find a job that contains all this? Does it even exist in real life? Is this just a pipe dream and an exercise in futility?"*

It's time to find out. Your prioritized needs now become the springboard for generating creative ideas for where you might find this work.

For an example of the idea generation process, environmental sustainability consulting director Annie was reviewing her prioritized values and struggling to come up with a new idea that excited her. Everyone seemed to covet her job, but she wasn't solving the problems or making the impact she wanted. Plus, for her Lifestyle pillar, she wanted more flexibility to work from home so she wouldn't have to spend so many hours commuting away from her toddler daughter. Annie had made a career change before, leaving the world of engineering for sustainability, and was hoping to leverage her past experiences to find a new path. As with many of us who have spent a few years in the working world already, she definitely didn't want to start over from the bottom or have to go get another degree.

How do you take all the desires from an individual and try to combine them into a new path? Imagine they're a chocolate cupcake. If we look at the recipe for making a fudgy, delicious chocolate cupcake with buttercream frosting, you'll find that you need flour, cocoa powder, eggs, butter, and sugar. Think of these as the main ingredients. If you want to try a new recipe with your baking, you can take some of the component parts and recombine them into something new, like a buttery chocolate croissant or a light-as-air eggy soufflé. The same ingredients in different combinations or ratios lead to lots of new, delicious ideas.

The same principle holds true for your career. For Annie, she had a love of solving nerdy, technical problems from her engineering and environmental consulting background, but wanted to make more of an impact on people instead of trees and rivers. She was interested in human psychology, optimizing performance, and managing individuals. When we started playing with her "ingredients" and looking at other recipes she could make, we started cooking up several fun ideas. One possibility that really sparked her interest was in product management: becoming the internal leader for development of a software project and coordinating different teams and stakeholders to create the best final product possible. When we began looking at organizations in the mental health and human performance space where she might be able to do product management, her Magnetic Interests, Strengths, and Lifestyle pillars really started to come together. She had informational conversations with employees at several organizations to feel out their company cultures and see where the right personality fit would be, and got an awesome offer as a product manager at a talent development software company where she could consistently work from home two days a week.

In the Career Clarity program, we work through an exercise called "Creativity Through Recombination" to generate opportunities for intersection. Essentially, you take brainstormed ideas based on your pillars and try to find new ways they could combine into possible roles. As you walk through the Creativity Through Recombination brainstorming process below, the most important thing is to focus on expansiveness and possibility. Quantity over quality. Don't censor or edit any ideas that come up yet because some of the most powerful information that comes out of these brainstorms is from the creativity found in weird or untraditional recombinations. While you might not want to be an "experiential marketing financial advisor" or a "food trend strategic analyst" or a “renewable energy operations manager,” which are all real combinations from past clients, these unique ideas might spark encouragement about new places to look for the role you would want. If you’d like help with organizing the Creativity Through Recombination exercise for yourself, go to GetCareerClarity.com/Bonus to get a free, printable copy of the companion worksheet.

To play with creative recombinations of your own prioritized pillar values, start by identifying your most important pillar. Each pillar has a corresponding trait in your ideal work that will lead your brainstorming process.

If your highest priority pillar is Strengths, you’ll start by brainstorming where to find possible roles that utilize your most important gifts. This is often the way we’re taught to think about career searching anyway, so this will probably be the most natural approach.

If your highest priority is Magnetic Interests, you’re going to brainstorm where to find the kinds of problems you want to help solve through your work. You’ll do this at a few levels: the department/team, the industry, and the organizations within the industry that intrigue you. Most career changers I’ve worked with have found that starting with team and working up, or starting with industry and working down to more granularity, are the most effective ways to approach this pillar.

If your highest priority is Personality, you need to brainstorm around environments, cultures, and teams that will align with you. This one is the trickiest one to start with. Sometimes starting with what you don't want (and where those unwanted traits are usually found) can help you brainstorm the kinds of organizations that would likely be free of the stuff you don't want — and full of what you do want.

If your highest priority is Lifestyle, then your mission is to brainstorm the industries and roles that can support the kind of lifestyle you're seeking. Remember that even humble-looking career paths can meet your financial and flexibility needs when you get creative, so be ruthless about your non-negotiables and incredibly flexible about how you can meet them all.

Let yourself go into a stream-of-consciousness state of pondering ideas. There's no bad idea, so even if you write down things like "professional trapeze performer" or "digital nomad influencer," getting possible ideas out of your brain and onto paper will help your creative juices flow.

Once you've generated at least 10 ideas under your highest priority pillar, brainstorm on your next highest pillar. Do this second round of brainstorming in isolation — without considering your top priority pillar — at first. Once you've created another 10 ideas here, start to look for places these ideas could intersect.

For example, Tyler may have decided that Strengths was their most important pillar, and completed a brainstorm of roles that align with their highest priority gifts. That sample brainstorm may come up with title possibilities like these:

Analyst
VP of strategy
Process improver
Efficiency consultant
Business process consultant
Idea generation facilitation
Strategy writer/developer

Then, since Magnetic Interests was their second highest pillar, they came up with these sector and industry ideas in their next brainstorm:

Startups
Health tech
Education tech
Mental health
Wellness
Individualized learning plans

Using creative recombinations, Tyler would try out possible intersections of strengths and interests to see what ideas seem spicy. Tyler might generate ideas like:

Startup efficiency consultant
Health tech idea generation facilitation

Individualized learning plan process improver
Education tech strategy writer
Wellness analyst

The goal in the exercise isn't to come up with the perfect job title. The goal is to show yourself what kinds of roles the world might need and to get ideas for the ones you'd most like to learn more about. From here, Tyler can create a short list of the creative ideas that spark the most excitement for them to explore further.

INTEREST		STRENGTH		POTENTIAL TITLE
Startup	+	Efficiency Consultant	=	Startup Efficiency Consultant
Health Tech	+	Idea Generation Facilitation	=	Health Tech Idea Generation Facilitation
	+		=	
	+		=	
	+		=	
	+		=	
	+		=	

Creativity Through Recombination is just one of many exercises to get your brainstorming energy going. Want to generate even more creative ideas? Try one of these tactics to discover additional paths.

Brainstorm "evolution" ideas: These are smaller-scale ways you can grow and evolve more naturally or incrementally from where you are now. This kind of brainstorming is most helpful when you have just one pillar out of alignment, and marginal improvement thinking can help wiggle in some fresh idea energy if you're feeling anchored in your current situation. Ideas might include ways to take on a new project, add responsibilities at your current job, or ask for small changes that could have big impacts, like more flexibility with your work hours or officially delegating a less enjoyable part of your job responsibilities. This is like switching from a chocolate cupcake with chocolate buttercream to the same cupcake with cream cheese frosting and sprinkles. It can be shocking what a big upgrade a small change can make! A client who did this masterfully made the shift from working for her company as a full-time employee to becoming a full-time contractor. You'll hear her full story later, but because Lydia's Lifestyle pillar was out of whack, by changing the terms of her employment, she was able to do work when she wanted and set new boundaries that let her spend more time with her partner and help him grow his guitar amp refurbishing business.

Percolate on "revolution" ideas: Get your brain thinking in a totally different way and explore possibilities that seem huge and outlandish. Quit your job and go to culinary school? Move to Kenya for two months on sabbatical? Go to law school? Start a nonprofit? Nothing is off the table if it aligns with your priority pillars. Thinking about quantum leaps and "flipping the table" ideas can help stretch your thinking. Maria is a great example of a revolution: she was a mid-career educator teaching biology to at-risk high school students in the Midwest, but had an itch to make a different kind of impact in her work. After talking about her revolution idea with friends privately for years, she decided to pursue her secret dream: becoming a doctor specializing in mothers and families in low-income areas. While it took her years to give herself permission to pursue her "revolution" as a mom to two young girls, when Maria got into medical school, she was thrilled. She'd spent years trying every other possible path to creating the impact she craved, like you'll learn how to do in Phase 2, and felt certain that leaving teaching and high schoolers behind was the right step for her.

Pretend to invite other people to your brainstorm: If your dad was looking over your shoulder, what ideas would he contribute? What if we invited Oprah, Bill Gates, or Michelle Obama to help you come up with ideas — what do you think they'd add? Challenging yourself to think like someone else can be a surprisingly effective tactic because it reminds you that you think more creatively than you give yourself credit for and helps use faux different perspectives to generate real fresh thinking.

Actually invite other people to your brainstorm: Know somebody creative or who loves tossing out ideas? Promise them a free latte or smoothie in exchange for poring over your 4 Pillars with you. Hearing an external voice coming up with ideas could be helpful in sparking your own creativity — or affirming the secret ideas you've had but were too afraid to articulate out loud. Pick someone who isn't in your closest circle: people who are related to you will often have conflicts of interest because they can sometimes think they benefit more from you staying where you are.

From here, Google will be your guide, helping you explore more ideas beyond what you've generated on your own. Try searching for "jobs for XYZ," inserting different combinations of your top pillar words and values, and see what comes up. Keep writing down the titles or ideas that speak to you.

Don't feel limited by title research alone. If your ideal fit role would be more of a combination, you're allowed to write down "restaurant owner + animal shelter manager + motivational speaker." Or "photography business owner + singer/songwriter" — a former Career Clarity coaching client actually created this in Florida. Or "nonprofit founder + project management consultant" like another client built in New Jersey.

For now, your goal is to get some directionally correct future career guesses going, not to find the exact title or job yet. We'll validate and flesh out your initial ideas more fully after following the steps outlined in Phase 2 of this process.

If you're feeling resistance to this idea generation work, take comfort that this stage is where people sometimes get stuck because they're falling into a common thinking trap: the "this won't work for me" trap.

It looks a little like your brain protesting, "*I'm not creative.*" Or: "*I've tried all the ideas already. There's nothing else out there for me.*"

When we're feeling frustrated and hopeless about our efforts, we tend to shift into extreme, black-and-white thinking — particularly my fellow recovering perfectionists. This all-or-nothing thinking takes away the ambiguous gray middle space where possibility, innovation, creativity, and hope all thrive.

Black-and-white thinking is adaptive and socially conditioned — it's not your fault. When the amygdala activates, the prefrontal cortex tries to rationalize the feeling by throwing this logic chain at us: *"If I'm sure that this idea won't work for me, then I'm already doing the best I could do right now. Therefore, if I do try something new, I'm opening myself up to looking like I'm doing a bad job or being criticized by others if they see I'm not perfect, so I better stay safe right here."* Miserable, but safe.

It's easy for our brains to convince us that unhappiness is better than uncertainty, because uncertainty doesn't feel safe.

But if you want to make a change, instead of resigning yourself to the unhappiness of staying in the same situation forever, you have to question everything. Every limiting belief, every subconscious agreement, every fear, and every time you shut a door to yourself in the name of managing your own expectations. In short, those tools we honed together in Chapters 4 through 7 will come in handy once again.

As you brainstorm ideas for your future career move, be willing to question the "buts" that pop up. Any hesitations or resistance are trying to help by keeping you safe, but if you let these beliefs act like facts and derail your momentum, you'll end up stalled out, frustrated, and stuck. Don't choose to stay stuck!

I can tell you the tale of two lawyers: one who was willing to question her "buts" and take action, and the other who was paralyzed by his limiting beliefs. Both wanted to pivot out of the soul-sucking litigation work they'd been doing, but neither was crystal clear on what would be next for them.

One lawyer was willing to question her belief that her juris doctorate would make it hard for her to find another job that paid what she needed. She did tons of informational interviews across law-adjacent roles in North Carolina and found that her soul *and* bank account would be delighted by seeking out policy roles in government or advocacy. Her belief that it was possible made Phase 2 a breeze because she could take action and reach out with ease.

The other lawyer was so bound by paralyzing fears that his previous work made him unmarketable that he wasn't willing to question those assumptions and talk to other lawyers (and non-lawyers) about the kinds of new roles his gifts made him well equipped to do. He was incredibly capable and passionate, yet convinced himself it was impossible to find another job he hated less than the one he was doing because he was sure he'd never make more money anywhere else.

Two humans, two similar backgrounds, two wildly different experiences based on how they decided to question their "buts" and approach their fears.

Let's lean into the next steps on your joy-seeking adventure together, and start seeing which of your ideas has potential to bring you career clarity.

CLARITY QUESTIONS:

What are 10+ aligned ideas generated from each of your 4 Pillars?

What are some possible ways your prioritized pillar needs can intersect in ways that would be joyful for you?

What are some steps you can take to generate even more interesting, exciting possible directions?

Phase 2

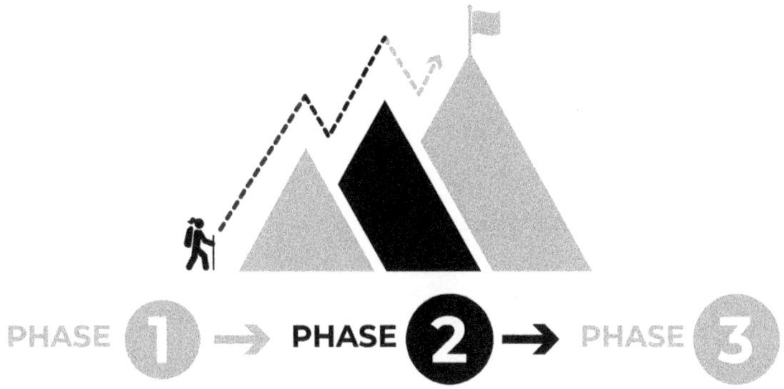

Congratulations on reaching Phase 2! At this point in your career exploration and joy-seeking adventure, you've created a handful of intriguing work ideas that are deeply rooted in the fabric of who you are and what matters most to you. By grounding your ideas in who you are, you're well on your way to a clear, exciting new career direction.

If we revisit our journey up Mount Fulfillment, you've decided on your initial route to trek up the mountain. You've got your backpack packed to perfection, you've prepared for the different conditions and terrain ahead, and you've calibrated your compass to always find true north. It's time to start testing your route to see if it can get you to the summit you want.

The initial excitement around coming up with compelling, aligned ideas is incredibly fun, especially for anyone who's a natural dreamer. Future possibilities give such hope and confidence about what's ahead of us.

At this point, traditional career resources would have you eagerly dusting off that resume and freshening up your LinkedIn profile — the equivalent of hiking straight up the mountain on the most direct route.

Those resources would be wrong.

While coming up with inspiring, motivating ideas is a great thing, it's also all hypothetical. You've thought up some possibilities that seem plausible but don't have real data points yet to confirm the reality is as great as the dream. Remember that sinking feeling in your stomach when you're dreading the day ahead? That's what we want to use a risk-managed strategy to avoid.

Imagine trying to walk straight up vertical cliff faces, or charging through a gooey swamp, or having to swim across a raging river you're totally unprepared for. Not only will you feel exhausted, you may also get stuck and decide that climbing the mountain isn't worth it, or that you'll never be able to do it.

The desire to take the fastest, most direct path makes sense on its face. Most of us have an anxious itch to "solve" or "finish" this career stuff once we've gotten a promising idea. We want to plant our flag on the summit and move into that new role as quickly as humanly possible. But that urge to be done pushes us to take shortcuts. It's the difference between "*I think this could possibly fit me...*" and "*I've done my due diligence and know this is the fit for me.*" One of those perspectives requires gathering critical data points to help you grow in confidence based on real experience. If you recall Chapter 5, we talked about how courage and commitment lead to taking the actions that develop your confidence and self-trust. We're about to watch that come to life right here in Phase 2.

Instead of jumping wide-eyed into breathlessly sorting through online job postings, we're going to take a test drive first. Trying out your possible new direction first is critical because it gives you experiential evidence that will clearly show you if the new career idea matches your expectations. It allows you to manage the risks inherent in making a change and validate your new direction — before you show up at the office for your first day. Think of this as doing a trial hike of your intended route up the mountain. You want to make sure your DEET-free bug spray is actually working, the area is mostly clear of weedy brush (or else you'll have to go buy a hiking machete), and there aren't any surprise rivers you can't ford.

This part of the process isn't as sexy or fun to talk about, which is why most career resources skip it entirely. It feels like it slows your momentum down.

My test drive definitely slowed me down. It was 2013, and I was anxious to figure out what was next for me after communications consulting. I was sitting on a seafoam green couch in my therapist's office — we'd been talking about my dissatisfaction at work and what other jobs I could do instead for a few weeks now. As I felt the glorious catharsis of word-vomiting my fears and dreams to another person, a new idea crept across my mind: *"I could do *this.*"*

Suddenly, I had a solution to all my career woes: take the GRE, enroll in graduate school, and make a huge career pivot into becoming a therapist. I loved sitting in my therapist's office for 50 minutes every other week, so why wouldn't I love becoming a therapist myself?

I became a woman obsessed.

I purchased my GRE study guide, started researching graduate programs' admissions requirements, registered for the exam, had my test date get snowed out, retook the exam, pre-wrote letters of recommendation for past bosses to sign and mail in, looked at my current company's tuition reimbursement policy, and wrote out my personal statement of intent. All within the span of three months. I hardly breathed between each step — I was desperate to make a change and get out.

One evening, I was carefully writing each part of the application for the Master of Science in Clinical Mental Health Counseling graduate program. I'd zoomed through writing answers to questions about my personal history and interest in pursuing counseling, and was on a roll. At this pace, I might even be able to send in my application early! But then, I scrolled to the next page of the application and stopped cold.

In front of my blinking cursor, I saw the section header for the next part of the application:

"RELEVANT TRAINING & COUNSELING EXPERIENCE"

My momentum skidded to an abrupt halt.

I could *kindof* fudge a few things I'd done in corporate to fit — I had, after all, run the mid-level manager enrichment program and received a lot of corporate management and leadership trainings — but at the end of the day, I had nothing truly counseling-like to include. As a former marketer and avid writer, I could spin up copy to convince people of just about anything… except this.

My intellectual integrity begged me to get some real-deal counseling experience I could add to my official grad school application instead of trying to embellish one of my corporate experiences. I grabbed my trusty laptop and started digitally sleuthing around for opportunities.

The question loomed in my mind: how does one get experience as a therapist?

There had to be a way, otherwise the application wouldn't have a question like that. But every time I ran another query through Google, my fears ramped up: who would let me get legitimate counseling work experience when I had none — and no credentials — to begin with? It felt like an impossible quest: everyone seems to want you to have experience before they're willing to give you an opportunity to get experience.

However, the more I searched, the more tiny possible opportunities started to pop up. While many employers want you to have significant relevant experience before taking a chance on you, everyone also knows that you have to start *somewhere.* It turned out that if you focused on volunteering and serving others for free in exchange for experience, people were surprisingly happy to give you opportunities to learn on the job.

Looking for volunteer opportunities is how I discovered an organization called Crisis Text Line. I'd been following their founder for years since her earlier nonprofit ventures, and had heard whispers that she'd just started this new organization.

Crisis Text Line is a text-based hotline for anyone in crisis. You text 741741 and receive a reply from a trained volunteer crisis counselor who helps you risk assess, de-escalate situations, and create a safety plan. It sounded awesome: super flexible, minimal hour commitment, and hands-on experience. And, even better: they were actively accepting volunteer applications.

I wrote my entire volunteer application in a single evening. As I approached the end, the final question of the application asked us to record a video about why we wanted to be a counselor. Nervously gulping down my fears about my lack of experience, I recorded my answer: I wanted to find a way to try this new thing and gain experience to help me decide if I wanted to go to graduate school. I hoped my enthusiasm and earnestness would be enough.

I pressed "submit" on my application, and waited. Held my breath. Crossed my fingers.

Three weeks passed, and then, a delightful ding in my email inbox announced: "Congratulations! You've been accepted into the Crisis Text Line crisis counselor training program."

If someone had mounted a camera on the wall, it would have seen me jumping around and fist pumping into the air. I excitedly sent emails to my mom, my friends, and my counselor about my acceptance — I did it! Or, at least I thought I had.

Once I'd completed the three-month comprehensive volunteer training program, I was ready to take my first shift as a certified volunteer crisis counselor. I logged onto the online platform for my four-hour volunteering slot on a Thursday night and had my inaugural text interaction. I nervously recalled my training, and helped coach that person on ways to move from their crisis situation into safety. Then, I took a second conversation and did it again.

After a few weeks of volunteering, I started noticing a trend: while I was absolutely loving supporting these texters each night, I was physically drained at the end of my shifts. Completely wiped. I'd start the shift feeling excited and nervous, and ended it so exhausted that all I could do was brush my teeth and roll into bed. And sometimes I didn't even have enough energy left to brush my teeth.

This volunteering was great, worthy work. It was helping people, it was impactful, and it was making a difference. But after realizing how exhausted and empty I felt after each volunteer shift, I realized that it wasn't the right fit for me. I couldn't imagine doing that work for eight hours a day, 40 hours a week, 52 weeks a year.

The clarity of this realization threw a giant monkey wrench into my perfect plan of volunteering, grad school, and epic career change. I wasn't supposed to be anything but over the moon about counseling. I was supposed to have resolved my career direction dilemma and be on my way to what's next.

The perfect dream of going to graduate school and becoming a happy therapist for the next decades of my career started to crumble.

What I thought "looked great on paper" didn't actually feel good in person. Back when I started my grad school application, I'd assumed that looking great on paper would be enough. It's not. This pesky assumption is why so many of us accidentally make mediocre-feeling career decisions — and why slowing down to take a test drive is so critical.

Phase 2 can be intimidating because it requires you to take action, bringing you face-to-face with all your fears about discomfort, failure, change, success, economic uncertainty, external judgments, and more. What it's critically important to remember is that research shows that fulfillment and meaning are inherently tied to growth, change, and stretching yourself. Conversely, "comfortable" is often where our soul will languish and atrophy.

If your Phase 2 test drive experience is anything like mine, you'll discover experiential data points that will help you determine what you do enjoy. For example, while volunteering on Crisis Text Line's online platform, I learned that working remotely was great for me. The trauma and emotional intensity of crisis counseling didn't feel good but making a difference for individuals was still important to me, which is what led me to explore career coaching. You don't gather the critically important data you need without letting yourself take a first step in your desired direction.

CHAPTER 15

Testing Your Potential New Career Paths

Now that you've got several seeds of ideas from your idea generation work in Phase 1, it's time to water those seeds and shove them in the sunlight to see if they sprout. Phase 2 begins with more brainstorming — this time, coming up with ways you can try a small-scale experiment to test if your career hypothesis could actually work for you.

This part of the Career Clarity framework requires you to cultivate a beginner's mindset. You have to be open to growth and change, and courageously put yourself out there to try things that are new to you. But don't worry — if you're feeling terrified about that level of vulnerability, working with fears around perfectionism or people pleasing is my specialty. I've got plenty of tools to help you take those baby steps, even when taking action feels more paralyzing than stumbling upon a grizzly bear smack dab in the middle of your path.

Let's use Anna as an example here: a woman working in Washington, D.C. who marched right up the corporate ladder in the publicity world and hit a comfortable salary and title with ease. There was something inside her itching and yearning for more: more soul, more challenge, more impact. She wanted more of a life and career on her own terms, instead of staying on the prescribed corporate ladder in front of her.

We got to talking about what "more" meant for her. After a few minutes of digging, Anna admitted that her heart's secret dream was to be a developmental book editor: the person who helps authors refine their ideas as they write books. She wanted the honor of being the idea doula, helping writers birth their big, bold, intellectual works into the world.

After she articulated her deepest desire to me out loud, the next morning Anna woke up with a feeling that I've started calling "the dream hangover." It's the *"oh, crap, I said WHAT?"* mix of regret, confusion, and fear.

Why do we feel hungover from sharing our vulnerable hopes with other people? It's because of that dang amygdala again. Fear jumps in and starts chastising us for sharing our dreams and believing they can happen.

Anna's innermost voice of fear was feeling left out of the conversation. Fear piped up and said, *"That was a fun fantasy, wasn't it? But let's talk about your real life. You could never make a change like that. You couldn't afford it, you're too old, and you're completely inexperienced."*

The arguments sounded compelling. If Anna believed that voice, she'd certainly stay safely where she was. But her heart, soul, and mind might never forgive her for neglecting their longing for challenge and expansion.

What that inner fear voice forgets is that every single book editor started out inexperienced at first. They all begin without the "right" credentials and, by taking baby steps of action to gain credibility and experience, methodically worked their way into the career.

There's no need to let your fear control your decision-making so you resign yourself to being part of the 47% of Americans who are actively unhappy in their work. You *can* have a job that aligns with your values, allows you to pay the bills, and that is fun for you.

Let's talk about Anna's amygdala and how she can start moving from feeling overwhelmed by fear to feeling grounded in hope and momentum. If even just 1% of Anna's heart believed that she truly could become a developmental book editor, what tiny actions could she take today to prove herself right and inch that belief up to 2%? Some ideas could be reading an article about a book editor or identifying her favorite publishing genres.

What if 10% of her believed this change was possible? What actions could Anna take to nudge that up to 11% of her heart and soul believing with all their might that she can do this? She could try taking a class on editing or reaching out to a famous editor to research their path into the industry.

And for all the marbles... what if 49% of her heart believed it was possible? What would Anna need to do to tip the scales in her favor and start a true momentum snowball? She might start by offering up her services to help a writer friend with their manuscript.

Your fear voice can be very helpful in specific situations, like we talked about in Chapter 5. It's great at keeping you safe and comfortable away from potentially dangerous risks. But when comfort and complacency are crowding out joy, growth, and adventure in your life, it's time to let fear take a backseat and let your heart's ambition drive.

What kind of career — and life — could you create if your heart was fully in the driver's seat?

Let's find out by strategically completing some small-scale experiments. By taking smaller risks now, you're actually setting yourself up to make a bigger, riskier transition more safely in the future.

There are two types of experiments you can run: tiny but meaningful "baby steps" and slightly more intimidating "up-the-ante steps."

Baby steps are the kind of actions that seem so small that you'd be forgiven for thinking they don't make a difference. They're the things you could almost do on accident or from your phone in bed late at night. Done intentionally, however, these information-gathering steps help you expand your knowledge into subject matter expertise in the area you want to possibly transition into.

Here are some example baby step experiments you could try, using your top priority pillar to lead the experimentation and research process:

> If **Strengths** are your biggest priority to get into alignment, a baby step could be doing some online sleuthing to see how people get into the kind of role you want. You can look up specific titles on LinkedIn, check out someone's professional profile, and see what certifications or trainings they did that allowed them to be successful in their current role. This can be particularly helpful if you find someone who's also a career changer and who's a few steps ahead of you on this journey. You could also take a free or inexpensive online class to learn a skill you want to develop to see if the idea of becoming an expert in that arena is as fun as the true process of getting there.

> If **Magnetic Interests** matter most to you, you can pick up a book about the industry you'd most like to be working in. Delving into background information on the sector's history, upcoming trends, and key players could be a good choice.

If your **Personality** fit is most important, you could chat up friends and former coworkers about the best boss or team they ever worked for. Ask questions about the traits that person had, how they identified them, where they're working now, and how they'd screen for a great-fit supervisor and company in the future.

If **Lifestyle** alignment is most critical for you, dive into online research about companies you're intrigued by and look at the information provided on their "Careers" page. What do they say about their standard-issue benefits and flexibility? Check to see if they specifically mention a particular perk you need so that you don't fall in love with an employer who won't honor your needs.

Similarly, the up-the-ante steps allow you to expand your knowledge even further. However, the key distinction between baby steps and up-the-ante steps is that the latter require you to get hands-on experiential knowledge about your potential future path. They need you to create a work sample, actually visit the workplace, and talk to other people about making your transition. They require more effort and more vulnerability, but they're the best way to affirm whether you like the career ideas you've generated.

Using your priority pillar to lead your up-the-ante exploration, here are some more intensive ways to try out a future path:

Strengths: Do a prototype work project to show off your capabilities. If you want to go into coding, set up a Github account and put sample code snippets up for people to review. If you want to be a copywriter, write a sample landing page or informational brochure for a company. Make the work product something tangible, and, even better, make it something that would actually help your target employer or someone in your ideal industry, so you could pass it along to them for review or use.

Magnetic Interests: Proving that the book learning you've done can translate into being a great employee can be tricky. As an example, former teacher Julia from Chapter 1 did this beautifully by creating a prototype podcast about experiential education strategies, effectively establishing herself as a budding subject matter expert. She reached out to leaders in the field and interviewed them on the podcast. Not only did she show off her own knowledge about the field, but she also created incredibly helpful, leveraged relationships with other thought leaders who could open doors for her in the future. You don't have to invest in a fancy microphone to up the ante on your interests: even just writing a few paragraphs about the state of the industry and publishing it on your preferred online platform gives future employers insight into your point of view on the sector and how you can help them.

Personality: Attend an event hosted by the organization whose culture you're curious about. A conference, panel, virtual happy hour, quarterly report release, or something similar can show you if you like the energy and personalities of the individuals you meet and help you get a sense for the company's cultural priorities.

Lifestyle: Do an informational interview with someone employed at a company you'd like to work for. Informational interviews are just a jargony way to say: set up a conversation with someone who has better first-hand knowledge than you about the organization and ask that person what you want to know about the real-deal company lifestyle. Do people tend to work past 6 p.m. on a regular basis? Do people take true vacations? Are there already people working remotely full-time, and if so, are they noticing that their professional growth is stagnating because of it? Asking someone at a company that doesn't have any jobs posted online can be great because that person will have no incentive to misrepresent things or paint a rosier picture. Plus, as you'll learn more about in Phase 3, there is a behind-the-scenes job market that you may be tapping into by reaching out proactively.

Before you put this book down today, brainstorm some small-scale experiments you could run to see how viable (and fun) your ideas might be in reality. It doesn't matter if they are baby steps or up-the-ante steps just yet. While up-the-ante steps might move you further faster, baby steps are great ways to start exploring a new industry and gain momentum to catapult you into up-the-ante experiments later.

The path to career clarity is paved with courageous steps and trying new things: write the blog post, start the podcast, take the class, meet the person in real life, shadow at the company. By themselves, none of these steps move the needle much individually. But combined, they build up to confidence, clarity, and a momentum snowball. Note that not everyone who goes through this process has an immediate "a ha!" moment when they discover their ideal career idea, so don't put pressure on yourself to have your own eureka epiphany before you've taken a significant number of baby and up-the-ante steps. Once you take action and find a path that feels like it truly fits you, you'll finally feel like you've found a clearing in the woods and a safe path to head up your mountain.

> " As you start to walk on the way, the way appears.
>
> Rumi

I have never seen a more courageous person navigating the fears around career change than Naomi, an administrator at a local hospital in Toronto. She was frustrated about being stuck in the same job for years without any room to grow, and felt uncertain as to where to go next. The stuck feelings were amplified because she was someone with an undergraduate degree in biology and health who'd already pursued a master's in radiology that hadn't panned out the way she'd wanted.

We mapped out Naomi's 4 Pillars and identified that her biggest desire was to work more in alignment with her strengths in communication, deep listening, caring for others, and helping people advocate for their needs. We brainstormed tons of possibilities together. After we'd generated 30+ different vocational ideas, from nonprofit program manager to social worker to healthcare copywriter, she realized her soul's dream was to work as a patient navigator: someone who helps patients and families communicate with healthcare providers through confusing, big, or scary decisions when they need intensive health support.

She was so moved by patient navigation that despite being a shy person, she courageously reached out to several current patient navigators to talk to them about how they liked their work. As she gathered data about what the job was like and how people landed their roles, she discovered a frustrating common fact: everyone she spoke to who was a patient navigator in the Toronto area had gotten there through a different healthcare role, like being a nurse, a healthcare reporter, or a social worker. Almost everyone had a health-related graduate degree, and as she looked at patient navigation job postings, most roles required it.

This academic speedbump was the ideal chance for her fear to take over and tell her that this career change would never happen for her because doing another degree would be expensive, time consuming, and high risk.

The "buts" came out big time. Instead of letting them derail her progress, she got curious and questioned the assumptions behind them. *"Do I have to do grad school to become a patient navigator? Would I actually enjoy the career one of these grad degrees might set me up with? If I focus on ways to make it happen, instead of on the obstacles, what can I see?"*

Naomi started to get curious about social work as a graduate path. She spoke with a few providers and ran into another big "but:" traditional social work required a lot of intense, emotional interactions that Naomi wasn't sure she was equipped to handle.

We questioned that "but." Was there a way to do social work that isn't as emotionally vulnerable and taxing? As she spoke to social workers, new, less taxing pathways started to appear: she could do case management work, become a policy advocate, or be a program manager at a nonprofit!

All of a sudden, going back to school to get a social services degree started looking like a great idea. It opened up tons of directionally-correct career possibilities for her in the short term and set her up to move toward patient navigation in the long term. She found a way to move forward through the "buts" that popped up, and, as of this book's publication, is currently completing credits towards graduation.

CLARITY QUESTIONS:

What are several small-scale experiments you could run to help vet your career ideas?

What is one baby step action you can do in the next 24 hours to test your potential career change?

What is an up-the-ante step you can plan on doing within the next month to confirm whether this is a good fit direction for your career?

CHAPTER 16

Evaluating Viable Options and Course Correcting

Once you've started taking baby steps and up-the-ante steps to try out your ideas, a critically important (and oft overlooked) part of the process is reflection. You spent so much time fleshing out your 4 Pillars that if you don't close the feedback loop and check in on how these options matched what you wanted, you're doing yourself a huge disservice. Without adequate reflection and course correction, most people struggle in this part of the journey because they feel like they're randomly throwing spaghetti at the wall and hoping that something sticks. If you don't diligently test hypotheses like a by-the-book scientist, you might accidentally create momentum toward a career path you don't love.

When you take the time to reflect on your small-scale actions, there are three possible outcomes. Knowing these possibilities ahead of time will help you set your expectations appropriately and know what to do next.

You try something out and you LOVE it. If you hit the nail on the head with your first guess for a new career path, fantastic! You'll probably feel excited, validated, or relieved that your test drive felt as good as you'd hoped. This most often happens when your 4 Pillars revealed themselves clearly to you and you've been sitting on a secret dream for a while without giving yourself full permission to pursue it. If you're feeling clear and confident on the career path you want to move into, keep hiking on this route and head right into Phase 3. A trail sign before you turn the corner: pay attention to why you've held yourself back on pursuing this dream before. Putting your finger on the reason will help you get past the real barriers and keep moving forward — whether it's a lack of confidence or fear of success and the disruptions and changes in folks' opinions of that you might follow. These fear or amygdala-related barriers are typically surmountable if you decide they are. Choosing to evolve from a timid trail hiker into a full-fledged explorer is simple, but not easy.

You try something and you like some parts of it but others violate your non-negotiables. If you try something gutsy for your up-the-ante and leave the test drive feeling mostly good but also a little concerned, this is probably you. Congratulations on putting yourself out there and trying something new! While you're processing the mixed experience you just had, it's important to pay attention to the elements that *did* work. It's easy to get bogged down in what didn't fit and doesn't feel good, but focusing on the negatives is the fastest way to take the wind out of your sails and convince yourself that there's no better job out there and you might as well stay stuck where you are.

Remember that the goal of the 4 Pillars framework isn't that you get every single pillar met perfectly and 100% in your next job — it's that you get the most important things right and trade off the less important priorities. It's feeling satisfied, not over-satiated.

To illustrate calculating ideal tradeoffs, let's talk about Lydia's story. After spending a decade in women's reproductive health access and advocacy, Lydia had thought she'd be satisfied in the industry forever, but was feeling completely burned out when we met. She knew that her current nonprofit healthcare management work fit some of her pillars well, because she was definitely solving problems that called to her, using her strengths, and liked most of her coworkers. However, there was serious lifestyle misalignment leading to dissatisfaction, burnout, and the fear she needed to change industries completely.

To address any slight misalignments, write down the things you've learned you want to keep in a future job. Then, write down how you wish the other, less ideal elements would have been. By articulating those wishes, you're already a step closer to finding work that will better fit you. From here, look at your Phase 1 idea brainstorm and add a new take to old ideas, using your newly clarified priorities and needs. Did the new information you gathered help you add more specificity or nuance to what you want? Let this be iterative: reflection and clarification are a repeated process for the vast majority of clients I've ever worked with. Only about 10% of clients hypothesize their new career correctly on the first try. Once you've recalibrated and landed on a new idea that better fits your pillar prioritization, come up with ideas to take a baby step in that direction to see if it feels more aligned. Each step you take is clarifying and helps you both take options off the list and add new, better fitting ones.

For Lydia, this iterative process meant trying a test drive to shift the way she structured her work. Instead of being a full-time employee for one organization, she tried out healthcare management work as a freelance consultant. She loved that she was immediately able to draw stronger boundaries with working hours, spend more time with her partner because she controlled her commute, and got to be more choosy about which projects she worked on. By changing the structure of the work, she upgraded the experience to be much more satisfying and lucrative.

*You try something and it *definitely* does not align with your 4 Pillars.* Of the three possibilities, this outcome is by far the most disappointing one. You try an idea because you hope it will be The One, and finding out it's definitely *not* The One can be heartbreaking. This happened to Mohammed, who wanted to create a business helping immigrant undergrad students land jobs at companies that paid for their work visas. While he was passionate about the cause, after he ran his test drives, Mohammed realized that he didn't enjoy helping with tactical resume and job search work at all.

If your test drive feels like a complete bust, most people's fear ramps up and starts telling them things like, *"Finding a fulfilling career will never work for me. This whole idea was unrealistic. I can't make a change. This was all for nothing."* All that amygdala activation from Chapter 5 kicks in once again to protect you from the disappointment, but derailing this defeated narrative is why your 4 Pillars are so darn important. The truth is that in order to do something fresh and new, you have to take some risks. Risks help you find out what works and what doesn't, and recalibrate your time and energy accordingly. You can reframe your inner fears and affirm your test drive by saying, *"Isn't it such a relief I did a small-scale experiment and found this out now, instead of actually getting the MBA, starting the business, or landing the job and realizing that I've made a grave mistake?"* You're using your best guess hypotheses to refine and clarify what matters most to you, and doing it faster and more efficiently than you ever have before. It makes sense your guesses aren't 100% perfect right off the bat — most people's first guesses need some refinement before they feel great — but you're learning helpful information so you can make better aligned choices.

> “Either I win, or I learn.
>
> Marie Forleo

Go back to your 4 Pillars and see where your guess was off or misaligned. What had initially made you think this idea would be good? Based on what you learned from your test drive, what do you need to update in your prioritization or process? Use this refined clarity and revisit Chapter 14 on idea generation and come up with some fresh ideas to give you new direction for baby step tests.

How did things turn out for Mohammed? He and his wife decided to create a pro bono mentoring program to give international students advice on effective job searches instead of doing the work for them. Mohammed revisited his fulfillment drivers to create a career within information technology leadership that better leveraged his energizing strengths, personality traits, and lifestyle needs. He designed a creative path that honored his interests in both his regular 9-to-5 and in his mentoring program, and let him feel soulful fulfillment. If you run a disappointing first test drive, be willing to keep testing and trying new possible paths like Mohammed until you find the one that fits.

There's one last experience you might have during this phase of your new career exploration: searching and searching online, looking for a role that seems built just for you but not seeing any job postings that look 100% like what you want. This happens when you've cultivated a clear sense of what the job ought to look like but can't find it in the marketplace.

If this is you, you have a bit of a courageous and inventive challenge in front of you. If you believe this work is worth being paid to do, your career vision might be inviting you to pitch this role to an organization. This is your equivalent of going off the marked trails on your mountain hike and trying your own creative route to the peak.

Your first step is to figure out what value this role would bring to an organization: the cold, hard numbers on how this work benefits a company's bottom line. How can your work allow them to make more money? Next, consider the kinds of companies that would most need a person like this. Who would benefit most from hiring someone with your specialty? Then, you're going to reach out to individuals at those organizations to gather their perspective on if they see a need for help on this problem, too. How are they currently addressing this need? How well is it working? How much is it costing them? From there, you can start planting the seeds that they need someone like you to fill this hole in their business strategy. This is a speedy quick overview of the pitching process, but if you're interested in covering this tactic in more depth, look out for the breakdown of strategic informational interviewing in Chapter 20.

Even if nobody has created quite the same career path as the one you want, there are always people who have scaled mountains before you who can help you figure out how to make it happen. You're not alone, and courageously asking for support along the way will always serve you. Lean into your courage and take action now to get the clarity and confidence you'll need to make your transition truly happen.

CLARITY QUESTIONS:

What have you learned from your baby steps or up-the-ante steps so far?

What was the most aligned and joyful option you've tried?

What else do you feel like you need to try to gain additional clarity and confidence?

CHAPTER 17

Managing the Bumps and Unexpected Bears On Your Journey

Remember Naomi, the aspiring patient navigator from Chapter 15? She's a shining example of what can happen when you dive into your Phase 2 exploration with abandon and question all your assumptions, but her story also illustrates the unexpected fears and obstacles that can pop up on your way.

After Naomi spoke with social workers, did her research, and felt confident she'd found a path forward that fit her 4 Pillars beautifully, she realized there was a bigger challenge standing between her and her ideal work. The trickiest issue of all: wanting full support and approval from her family.

Even though Naomi was deeply unhappy in her energy-draining administrative job, she knew her family wouldn't agree with quitting to get more relevant experience for her social services graduate program application and focus on school full time. Even though she had the financial runway to follow through on her plan, they were convinced she was becoming unemployable and would never succeed in school.

Phase 2 could also be called the Courage Phase: the fears that pop up about change, including the prospect of losing support and approval from family, are one of the scariest parts of finding work that fits who you truly are.

When you're little, grownups tell you things like, "*You're too shy to ever do public speaking*." Or, "*Nobody makes a living as a professional cello player*." Or, "*In our family, everyone who is successful becomes a doctor or a lawyer*." Hearing statements like those as a child — a wee babe whose prefrontal cortex isn't fully developed and can't use its full executive function to separate fact from opinion — means you received most early opinions as if they were facts. It can be really difficult to grow beyond those "facts" when you're an adult trying to forge your own path.

Imagine being weighed down by the fear that you'll never advance into leadership or success simply because an adult once called you "too bossy" or "too shy" as a kid. Or, being told that because you were born a woman, or black, or Muslim, being wildly ambitious is not what "we" do.

As adults, we get the privilege of taking actions to combat every time we were told we weren't enough. Our lives — and living them on our own terms — can be our greatest revenge. Our agency and choices can be the greatest healing salve for our deep-seated fears.

We have to be aware enough to see what's happening and make a new choice. For example, if you grew up in a painful and limiting situation, some of those core fears might be on replay in your career.

Maybe you lived with a parent who constantly blamed you for all their problems because they rarely took responsibility for their mistakes. Their narcissism or abdication of responsibility could have made the child version of you feel like you're never good enough and don't deserve love. Today, you seem to always end up with bosses who have anger issues, and every time you've been passed over for a promotion, you assume you need to put your head down and work even harder. If any of this feels familiar, you'd be shocked how many other people put intense "striving" energy — constantly pushing yourself to do more, be better, work harder — into their careers due to a fear of losing love and approval.

Maybe your family struggled with money insecurity throughout your life. The trauma and embarrassment of never knowing if you could afford new clothes or a school lunch left you focused on building your career toward bigger and bigger paychecks. You may now have a job that's externally impressive to other people, but you're working yourself to the bone and are terrified of being fired… and feel like you've given up all hopes of happiness or finding work in accordance with your morals. Trying to make a career change might seem like the logical thing to do, but you may still have some fears about financial security that you just can't seem to shake.

Maybe your story is about growing up with a family member who battled substance abuse or was chronically ill. You racked your sweet little kiddo brain for ways to help them, leaving you as the constant caretaker and feeling guilty for having any needs or desires of your own. So now in your work, you might be the office martyr, suffering because of others' poor project timelines and scope creep. Boundaries become blurry when you're a fixer, and your over-giving leaves you so tired it feels almost impossible to advocate for boundaries, fair compensation, or taking time off. Thinking about leaving and switching careers, even though you know it will make you far happier, makes you feel guilty or ashamed.

Even positive origin stories can have tricky consequences in our careers. You might have grown up in an incredibly loving and supportive household where you were always praised for being helpful. If you were known as "Grandma's little helper" and loved being known that way, notice if that reputation has carried over into a need to put yourself second in a never-ending desire to be of service and helpful at work. Fears of changing away from your beloved early identity can keep you stuck, even when you rationally know that continuing to be the best selfless helper displaces other things that are important to you.

Our family of origin stories can play out in our careers unconsciously. We look for work that gives us that feeling of being enough, being safe, being lovable, being important, or being visible. But when we've flown the nest and seeking those feelings through work just creates more pain and pressure, it's time to stop making career choices influenced by fears of old experiences. Childhood beliefs can put immense pressure on work to be much more than a job, and often make your work responsible for your emotional well-being in unhealthy ways.

Real fulfillment and peace come from taking the pressure off work to be the silver bullet that "fixes" everything that feels out of whack in our lives. Finding the "perfect" job won't be the solution to your fears — retraining your brain is. Your past doesn't have to be your destiny. Choosing to look at all the factors that influence the kind of work you're seeking and what you value is a powerful step toward finding work that's actually enjoyable and sustainable.

By the time you get to Phase 2, you most likely have identified at least a couple new directions to explore.

For some people, the real roadblock here is that your early brain was taught that staying small and staying stuck is safe, and taking action to explore new options threatens your ability to have the love, approval, or financial security you crave.

In this world of almost limitless abundance, it's strangely easy to be content with a less-than-ideal reality. Even though it seems like there are a zillion "how-to" guides and it seems almost impossible that you'd fail if you try, risk feels threatening because fear tells you there's a chance of failing. It's a pretty darn small chance, but it's there. But on the other hand, it's easy for the amygdala to overlook the huge risk in staying where you are.

Creating a career path that you want — and actually getting the perks and flexibility available to you — takes more than information.

It takes guts in the face of fear.

By having the courage to take ownership of what's next for you, you become fully responsible for your successes and your lessons. Taking accountability for picking up the pieces if something doesn't go perfectly can feel scary as heck. Willingness to take a risk — even a calculated, thoughtful, strategic one — is inherently a wee bit terrifying. But if there's one thing everyone I've encountered has in common, it's this: we consistently underestimate our own resilience. We are far more capable than we give ourselves credit for.

If you're struggling to take action on your baby steps or up-the-ante steps, take a moment and bask in the accomplishment that is you finally making a gutsy move and working toward the kind of career you've been dreaming about. Envision the next steps: where will you be two years from now? Would you be managing a team of employees you love, getting paid what you're worth? Or would you be in a jungle coworking space in Bali, sipping on a fresh coconut, doing international conference calls through your computer?

How would that feel? Who would you be if you started taking action toward building that future for yourself?

> “Your new life is going to cost you your old one. It's going to cost you your comfort zone and your sense of direction. It's going to cost you relationships and friends. It's going to cost you being liked and understood. But it doesn't matter. Because the people who are meant for you are going to meet you on the other side. And you're going to build a new comfort zone around the things that actually move you forward. And instead of like, you're going to be loved. Instead of understanding, you're going to be seen. All you're going to lose is what was built for a person you no longer are. Let it go.
>
> Brianna Wiest

What kind of progress can you make on those dreams if you have the guts to get started today? That's the real risk — delaying making a decision to take any action until you feel 100% "ready." It's a trap we fall into every day: we forget that deciding to delay is a choice, too. But we never really feel completely ready to take courageous actions. There's no such thing as the perfect time to make a change in your life.

My own career transition started in 2013, but I didn't successfully launch a business until 2015. I needed two full years of trying things, messing up, starting over, and learning until I could successfully start and grow a profitable business. And I didn't end up fulfilling my dream of drinking from a coconut while working from Bali until 2017.

None of it will start if you don't.

Envision that new job, that new career, that digital nomad dream, that move to Thailand, that new business. Let yourself relish that vision of where you could be in two years — even if it feels unreasonable.

If you take an action step toward your career dream and it doesn't work out perfectly, you've still started to generate momentum and clarity about what "success" looks like. For most of my clients, missing the mark was one of the best things that ever happened to them because it taught them about their scrappiness and ability to pivot. Their biggest disappointments end up being the most important lessons learned and create opportunities for more future joy.

The people in the world who love their work are the ones who felt fear and took action anyway. Started before they were ready. Reminded themselves that sometimes fear is a false alarm. Decided the idea of growing into their more empowered, confident selves is a road worth traveling.

If you're finding yourself feeling stuck or resistant to trying something without knowing if it will turn out right, remember that your joy and fulfillment are worth fighting for — especially when work occupies more time in your life than anything else you'll do for the majority of your lifetime. This is another place where perfectionism may be limiting how you think about creative, low-risk, easy ways to test your ideas.

Don't let fear of a change make perpetual unhappiness more appealing than temporary uncertainty.

Your mountain is waiting for you. You know what kind of freedom and fulfillment are available to you if you can take courageous steps beyond your fears. You've taken the time to test your course through all your baby steps before. It's time: you're ready to climb.

CLARITY QUESTIONS:

Are there any stories you learned when you were young that might make it tricky to take action on changing your career?

If you take action, where could you be two years from now?

What would it mean to feel fear and take action anyway? Who would you become?

CHAPTER 18

Deciding to Go Your Own Way and Explore Entrepreneurship

You might be reading through Phase 2 and thinking to yourself, *"I've brainstormed potential directions for me, and I'm not seeing anything in traditional employment that excites me. I've spent the last years zooming up the corporate ladder, consistently outshining my peers, and keep feeling called toward something more. I'm entrepreneurship-curious. What if I want to start my own thing instead of working for someone else?"*

Ambitious and analytical individuals like you love the idea of entrepreneurship because you can see the market opportunity. One compelling statistic about starting your own business is that there are more than 35,000 single-person businesses in the U.S. making more than a million dollars a year. If this sounds intriguing to you, I'd guess you may or may not have whipped up a business plan in Excel for fun on a Friday night.

If that's you, Phase 2 is going to be your sweet spot, because the best thing to do if you're considering self-employment is test it out with small-scale experiments.

It's true that running your own business can be a fabulous option to help you pivot your career and use your strengths to get more fulfillment out of your work. But while your heart might be aching for the freedom of working for yourself, your brain might go into risk management overdrive when you start to think about making a bold change like striking out on your own and starting your own business, even if you're an ambitious, analytical, go-getter.

Taking the leap into the uncertain world of entrepreneurship is scary, so it's normal that your fear is trying to pull your brain's emergency brake. You might recognize these fear-filled whispers from your inner self-doubt or fear voice once again: *"What if you quit your job today and don't get any traction in your entrepreneurial endeavor, go completely broke, liquify all your investments, have to break your lease, and move back in with your parents?"* Or worse: *"What if you put so much pressure on your dream that you suck the fun right out of it, and entrepreneurship becomes even worse than working for someone else?"*

These fears make total sense. The stakes of what's at risk are high!

Your inner project manager — the voice that says, "We're over budget on lines 2, 7, and 12" — wants to keep you safe, and it knows that being an employee seems a lot more stable and secure than entrepreneurship. That voice might try to convince you that staying employed is the only "responsible" thing to do when you have a spouse, a mortgage, or kids in the financial equation.

But settling into the safe, known, and comfortable path for the rest of your life could be a one-way ticket to Complacency and Boredomville, USA. You don't want to live the next decades knowing you're capable of more and never giving yourself a chance to find out what you can do.

But instead of telling you to quit your job on Friday and start your business on Monday, I want to give you different advice. If you leap, the net won't always appear. Don't jump directly into full-time entrepreneurship… yet.

Not making a dramatic, sudden pivot into full-time self-employment isn't a cop-out: it makes good financial sense and manages risk. Even if you're ready to abandon the corporate ship this afternoon, it might not make the most sense for you to quit today without having started building your business. You don't want to quit your job, try entrepreneurship on your own from scratch, and find yourself on your therapist's couch a month later talking about managing overwhelm, guilt, and paralyzing fear. Instead, let me share a secret passage to entrepreneurship that balances the risks with financial responsibility. It's called a "bridge" job.

In the book *Pivot* by Jenny Blake, a bridge job is defined as a new job, usually working for someone else, that moves you toward your dream of entrepreneurship by letting you hop to a directionally correct lilypad — the one that's right between full-time employee and full-time entrepreneur.

There are tons of possible ways to engineer a satisfying bridge job, including:

- Leapfrogging into a job similar to your current one, but in the industry you want to become an entrepreneur in
- Moving into a new role in your current organization that equips you with more of the knowledge, relationships, or skills you'll need to work on your own
- Pulling what researcher Emilie Wapnick coined as an "Einstein" in her book on multipassionate individuals: move into a job that doesn't require 100% of your brain or energy from 9-to-5, so you can lean back from your full-time job and lean into building your side hustle in the 5-to-9 hours
- Transitioning into different/alternate working hours, whether that's four 10-hour days a week or moving into official part-time work, to free up time and space to build your business.

What's amazing about a bridge job is that it allows you the stability of a predictable paycheck and benefits while you're acquiring the skills and resources you need to go full-time in your new business. If you play your cards right, you can set boundaries on your bridge job work hours that give you the flexibility to start building your new business deliberately and methodically on nights and weekends.

Even more amazing? You're not putting a ton of pressure on your baby business to become your full livelihood overnight. Less pressure means you'll have more fun building it slowly part-time until it's making enough money that you can transition your employment to part-time or become a full-time entrepreneur.

A bridge job helps you set a precedent of choosing a path that feels good to you in multiple steps, instead of making a huge jump too quickly. When you're the boss full-time in your new business, you want to feel like you know how to take strategic and calculated risks rather than feeling like your transitions are gigantic and terrifying.

If this path sounds like it manages risk well, the next question becomes: how can you create or find the ideal bridge job to fit your needs?

Your mission is to move into a job that is more fun, helps cross-train you for your future business, and allows you to draw boundaries so you have plenty of energy to build your new company on the side. To fit all three criteria, you need to create a vision of the business you want to build so you can tell if a potential bridge is directionally correct for you or not. If you're enthusiastic about nutrition education, getting a bridge job working at FritoLay may not be the right fit for you unless it's helping you fill other critical gaps in your skill and knowledge toolbox.

The first step toward identifying your ideal bridge and coming up with workable, fun business ideas is looking back at the strengths you mapped in Chapter 8. While all your pillars will be helpful in this process, it's usually easiest to start with your strengths and the gaps you might want to fill before going out on your own.

Moving into a corporate job that doesn't use your strengths is a recipe for burnout and frustration — and building a company that doesn't leverage your strengths is an even worse idea for your future happiness. So if you're wanting to build that nutrition education business and have a gift for one-on-one conversations, you probably won't be happy in a bridge job doing software engineering.

Your strengths are where your most marketable superpowers lie, so knowing them is the foundation of your success as an employee and as a budding entrepreneur. That means you must use your strengths to find that great bridge job and future business idea. If you don't, you might end up right back where you started: overworked, resentful, and unhappy with your job and life.

The experiments in Phase 2 will help you find bridge work ideas that use your energizing strengths, are in alignment with your personality, solve problems you're interested in, and allow you to create your ideal lifestyle. Finding these traits in your bridge job will build a stable, strategic step towards what's next so you'll never look back.

For an example of a successful bridge job transition, let's look at Jake. Jake in Ohio majored in engineering, and after a short and unfulfilling stint in teaching, he went into engineering management full time. He had a secret dream to be an entrepreneur, but didn't know how to take the first step to bring it to fruition. We looked at his 4 Pillars, honing in on his strengths to start generating initial ideas. He saw an exciting possibility in independent consulting and teaching, but also identified a skill gap in his ability to know how to do sales and business generation. Through working together, Jake created a path to more career fulfillment by become an intrapreneur: he found a bridge job opportunity within his current company and made a joyful transition into new business project management. The role let him continue collaborating with his former colleagues while also learning about how to find and cultivate possible business leads. At the same time, he started doing free consulting work on the side to build a portfolio of results and generate awesome testimonials about his work. When we last spoke, Jake had acquired a business partner and was creating a second stream of steadily growing income that could enable him to leave his job when he was ready.

Once you've secured a bridge job, you can start building your future business on the side. This is exactly what I did when I worked at my last job before becoming a full-time entrepreneur: I would work from 9 a.m. until 5 p.m. for them, and then work from 5 p.m. until 9 p.m. for me. It took me just over a year to ramp up the side hustle while working my bridge job, and growing the business slowly meant that I had time to test and validate lots of ideas in a risk-managed way.

If you're intrigued by entrepreneurship, experiments that can help you test drive it include offering your future business service to someone for free to gain experience, doing a reduced-price beta offering to see if your idea has market viability, developing your unique positioning statement to show how you're different from other businesses, or creating a first tiny batch of your products and selling them to friends or family. Getting proof of concept — and establishing what the lean project management world calls your "minimum viable product" — is key to helping you identify your market, your business model, and the skill gaps that a bridge job might help you close.

CLARITY QUESTIONS:

Do you feel like entrepreneurship could be the ideal fit for you?

What kind of directionally correct bridge job seems like it could help you fill any gaps before you go out on my own?

How will you create some consistent protected time to try small-scale experiments to validate your business idea before you make the full leap into running your own business?

Phase 3

Let's check in: how have your test drives and baby steps been going?

If your small-scale experiments left you feeling clear and confident on your route up Mount Fulfillment, keep on trekking! You're ready to transition from Phase 2 to Phase 3, where you will learn and employ the most effective strategies to summit the career mountain.

If you're not sure where you are on the mountain or whether you're ready to head for the top, let's reorient you on what you've done so far and where you're headed.

In Phase 1, you mapped out who you are and what you value most to identify work that would fit you. You dissected each of your 4 Pillars of Career Fulfillment in depth, and after prioritizing your non-negotiables, you brainstormed a few possible career directions that align with your fulfillment drivers. You completed this phase with a short list of career options to research.

In Phase 2, you've tested your ideas against reality. You identified the biggest questions about whether a career path would fit you, and then took baby steps or up-the-ante steps to try out your desired path to see how it felt. You've gained a ton of new information in Phase 2, including informational (research, online sleuthing, taking classes) and experiential (conversations with people who already do the role, job shadowing, creating thought leadership) data points. You'll know you've completed this phase when your test drives are complete, you've gained lots of new insights, and you've narrowed in on one exciting idea to pursue.

Everything you've learned up until now has given you further clarity, energy, and momentum on your career change journey. Now you've got a real, lived sense of what fits you, which means you're gathering more momentum and getting ready to start your official job search.

At this point, it's time to take all that confidence and conviction you've created and move from Phase 2 to Phase 3. Here, you'll learn the critical components of making a career shift successfully: proof that you're serious about your career change (which you generated in Phase 2), a sparkling new professional brand focused on where you're headed instead of where you've been, and a warm and wonderful web of strategic relationships.

Provable experience highlights any relevant hands-on experience you have that's not captured in your current work history, and ensures that hiring managers treat your application seriously. Great branding makes the story you tell about yourself as a candidate match up with the direction you want to go, not the career you are trying to leave. Strategic relationships give you opportunities to tell your story yourself by interviewing for unlisted jobs instead of languishing in the black hole portal of doom otherwise known as online applicant tracking systems.

A weird experience seems to pop up almost like surreal clockwork when folks follow the framework in Phase 3: your old life tries to tempt you back into staying. I have countless examples of clients who started to get really excited about a new career direction, and then out of nowhere, their current bosses suddenly bestowed promotions, raises, bonuses, and new projects on them. The shiny new opportunities at your old job seem awfully tempting, even when you're sure you are 100% committed to leaving.

If this happens to you, stay strong. Unless these dangling temptations truly align with your 4 Pillars in a way that's sustaining — and not just a temporary Band-Aid — you'll be better served by continuing to explore what's next. With that, let's enter the final phase of your Career Clarity journey.

CHAPTER 19

Positioning Your Job Search in the Right Direction

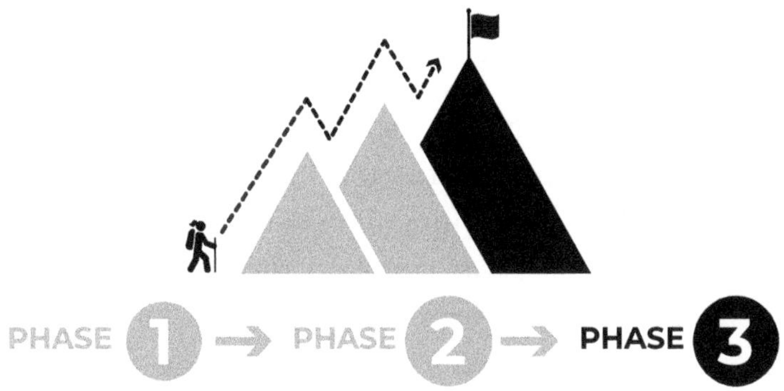

Once you've completed the first two phases of the Career Clarity framework and set your sights on the ideal next step, Phase 3 can legitimately be a piece of cake (or a chocolate cupcake). While job searching feels overwhelming and frustrating when you're not clear on what you're seeking, it's surprisingly intuitive and even fun when you know who you are and what you want. Your mission now is to play all out, and go all-in on an effective, strategic job search game plan.

To understand how to craft an effective and strategic job search plan, it's important to know the trends that are shaping the job market. This can help you both see when the tried-and-true tactics will work, as well as reasons why the advice you might have gotten from your parents or grandparents won't be relevant to job searching today.

First, let's look at workforce-level trends to understand other job seekers' behavior. One study that's important context for your search is the yearly study from The Freelancing Union and Upwork. Based on their most recent study, more than 50% of the entire American workforce will be freelance or have freelanced by 2027.

If you're not planning on freelancing, you might be wondering why this matters. Whether or not you personally end up working independently, this study shows that the way we compete for work is shifting — and how organizations compete for talent. Because there's mounting proof work can be done effectively remotely, employers are going to be comparing costs and capabilities of full-time role applicants to possible freelance counterparts anywhere across the nation. Employers may start offering more flexibility and perks to woo people away from freelance work, or they might start offering fewer benefits and more short-term project contracts. Open opportunities will have more local and national competition. No matter how the workforce and employment shift, you're going to need to know how to stand out and differentiate yourself in a whole new way. The two most important tools to help you stand out are leveraged strategic relationships and a unique professional brand. From here on out, you need to think about relationships and effective branding as precious, non-negotiable assets for landing your next job.

Why are these two assets more important than advanced degrees, new certifications, or a professionally designed resume?

The Bureau of Labor Statistics has reported for years that around 70% of job offers come from relationships — not from online applications. To make matters even trickier, depending on which study you reference, between 40-80% of job openings are never made publicly visible on a company's "Careers" webpage. This "hidden" job market doesn't always refer to the secrecy of the job opening, but rather to the process of finding employees in an unadvertised way.

The implications of these two statistics are big:

1. If you want access to the secret part of the job market where up to 80% of jobs are hiding, insider relationships are the only way to find it.

2. If you're only applying for roles that are visibly posted online, you've been accidentally limiting your employment prospects and aren't giving your brand the best chance to shine.

3. Your parents were right: there are things more important than just what's on the internet.

Crap crap crap, right?

If your job search strategy has solely consisted of looking at virtual job boards and applying online, you're competing with literally thousands of other people for the tiny percentage of hires that come in as cold, external candidates. The online job board game means you're praying you've put something in your cover letter or resume that a bleary-eyed human resources screener will magically see as a diamond in the digital rough. It's kind to call this strategy a long shot. It isn't that it will never work, but it does mean a heck of a lot of elbow grease. It would be a lot easier on you if someone at the company walked over to the job's hiring manager and said, "I met this person who has a great story, and we should bring them in for an interview."

To add even more emphasis to relationship building: the more competitive or "sexy" the company is, the more likely they don't do external hiring without an internal referral.

You read that right. The more coveted the brand, the more likely they only consider job candidates who come with a sparkling recommendation from a current employee. Given that top companies can receive thousands of applications for open roles, screening for referrals is one of the only ways they can sift through the massive pile of potentially strong applications to find the ones that current employees approve of — and are willing to put their own reputation on the line for.

It's another potentially frustrating hurdle between you and a great new job. But instead of getting mad and force-quitting all your open online job application tabs, let's upgrade your strategy for job hunting together.

The first necessary condition for successful job searching is "product" differentiation and a strong brand.

To think about product differentiation, let's use an example from the retail world. Outdoor clothing companies like Patagonia and The North Face offer similar jackets, hats, and hiking boots, but found ways to differentiate their brands so consumers don't treat all jackets the same and shop solely on price. If you know anybody who's into hiking and mountain sports, they likely have a favorite brand between the two, and probably have an impressive display of brand loyalty inside their closet. In the same way, you have to think of yourself as a product needing a unique brand to appeal to your target employer.

Online job application portals make it so that thousands of people can submit their resumes for a single job with the click of a button in what's colloquially called the "spray and pray" job application approach. The average online job posting receives hundreds of applications, and nearly half a million people post their resume on Monster.com every week. To be in charge of your next career move, you need to make yourself stand out from the crowd.

How can you show your ideal employer that you're well worth an interview? It's all about how you tell your story of who you are as a candidate — and crafting a compelling narrative about being a career changer that you can confidently share in interviews, cover letters, resumes, online profiles, and more.

One of the biggest challenges is that a lot of the points you may want to include in your narrative come from what you've done before, not what you want to do next. If we tell your story exclusively using your past moves from job to job, it will be hard for future employers to get excited about your career pivot. Instead of telling a linear story rooted exclusively in the past, the trick to differentiate yourself is to write a forward-looking "soul story" that paints an inspiring picture of the future.

A soul story, a concept borrowed from writing coach Kat Short, is an approach to talking about yourself that revolves around three core questions: Why, How, and Now.

When you talk about your Why, you help explain your mission and vision behind making a change. What's your motivation for switching career paths? What are you craving more of in your life? What's the driving force behind your work? This story should be born from the excitement that you have around making a change and how it aligns with your values so people can connect your values with their own.

Then, the How addresses the way this mission has been a part of your life in the past and present. You can share the story of your transition and all the cool things you did in Phase 2. Had incredible, life-changing informational interviews? Created prototype work products you're proud of? Talk about them here so someone can see how you live the truth of your why in your daily life.

Finally, the Now addresses what you're looking for moving forward. What kind of opportunities do you want next? What would help you get there? This can often include asking for specific advice or help, or simply stating the objective you're out to accomplish like making connections in the microfinance industry, finding a mentor in venture capital, or securing a job where your background can support a growing tech startup as their director of product.

> "Using the Why, How, Now method, you give people multiple access points to connect with you and continue the conversation. After all, most impact begins with an idea or spark and then, critically, a conversation. Voicing your story is how you make things happen. You can't just keep it to yourself, you must tell your damn story.
>
> Kat Short

Once you've told the story of how you arrived at this moment and what you're looking for in a way that's more compelling, engaging, and human than the linear "past jobs" approach, you've got to test it out to make sure it resonates. This brings us to the tactical execution of your story-forward job search approach.

Execution can be challenging, and thrilling when you get it right. For an example, Chiara is an excellent case study of changing your personal brand narrative to make it more soulful. Chiara worked in a sales role for a library services company. She'd been there for seven years, had done practically every single job on the sales team, didn't love her work anymore, and was desperate to get out. Her dream? Work in sales retention and account management for a recognizable software-as-a-service (SaaS) tech company. But Chiara was sending out application after application without getting responses. She was getting some traction, but it was only on front-end sales roles that she was uninterested in.

When our paths crossed, she was feeling hopeless and deflated. In our first conversation, I dug in: "What are you feeling most scared about?"

"I'll never be able to get into the tech industry with my current resume," she said. "I can't get a job in SaaS without experience, and I can't get experience without already having the job. I'm totally stuck." Based on her results so far — lots of traction for jobs she'd already outgrown or didn't want — it was clear that this felt like the truth. But it didn't have to be her truth.

"What if we tell your story differently?" I pondered. "You want to work at a software-as-a-service company but have no software experience. But you do have service sales experience." This was her How.

I asked, "What if the story you tell is focused on how you know how to sell services? That the feature that truly differentiates software products is how people experience the service of it? And we can even work in your background: the fact that you've worked in every role on a sales team means that as the account manager, you'll know exactly when to pull in the other team members for retention risks, addressing product bugs, or supporting the client team with onboarding."

Same human, totally different narrative — and completely different confidence level. Chiara rebranded herself using truthful information about her background, presented in a newly upgraded and compelling way. She used this new approach to revamp her resume and share her newfound confidence and clarity with recruiters.

For an example of rebranding to address a different challenge, let's look at Sam, an awesome senior associate at a top-tier consulting firm in Washington, D.C. She had a resume that would make people drool over its extensive list of accomplishments, but she'd hit a growth ceiling and was facing the double whammy of burnout and bored-out. Despite her shining list of capabilities and accomplishments, she wasn't getting responses from the jobs she wanted most.

We took a look at the way she presented herself on paper. It was impressive… and overwhelming.

Her resume was so chock-full of accolades that there was hardly any white space. She'd certainly done a lot, but by including so many bullet points it was hard to tell what she specialized in. Studies show that recruiters and HR screeners tend to spend 15 seconds or less reviewing your resume, so if they can't quickly and clearly see your zone of genius on paper, they'll assume you aren't worth their time and move on to the next.

Resumes are tricky, no matter what, because each industry, role, and country has different expectations and norms. For this situation, our solution was to streamline her story by cutting the number of resume bullets she had in half. The only ones we kept were the ones that were impressive, important, and relevant to hiring managers for the jobs she wanted most — most connected to her Why and How. By making her more focused and measured (at the expense of looking incredibly well-rounded), her response rates for applications skyrocketed. She told me: "I've gotten a call back for every single job I've applied for since I started using your instructions." By making such a simple tweak to her branding, she scored a job she was excited about with a 45% pay increase.

In an increasingly competitive job market — and when you have an untraditional background — branding matters. Taking time to articulate how you stand out, and why your past experiences make you a unique asset will help you not only land jobs, but negotiate handsome job offers.

CLARITY QUESTIONS:

What are your "Why, How, and Now?" What could your "Why, How, and Now" soul story be? How does it feel when you share it?

What are the most important and relevant accomplishments from your past career experiences to share?

What actions did you take in Phase 2 that you can talk about as helping you gain applicable expertise?

CHAPTER 20

Building Effective and Strategic Professional Relationships

The other component of upgrading your job search game is building strategic relationships — but let's think about relationship development in a completely new light. I hardly even use the dreaded term "networking" anymore because it evokes images of power suits and perma-scowls in a stuffy underground bar with people pushing their business cards on you and asking, "So what do you do?" Nobody wants to sign up to do that over and over again if they can help it.

If you think about relationship building differently, it can completely transform the actions you take. I always frame networking as strategic (so it's intentional and thoughtful) and as making professional friends (so it's focused on relationship building and genuine connection). Either of these definitions allows you to leave those dimly lit, awkward networking happy hours behind.

A big hesitation people have about the relationship-first informational interview approach is the amount of time it can take. They're afraid that if they don't apply soon-quickly-now, someone else will snatch the role away from them, or nervous that their attempt at relationship building will be a time-intensive flop.

Both of these fears are valid, so let's address each. If you wait a few business days to send your job application while looking for a contact and the posting expires before you apply, you probably were an underdog anyway. Why? Job postings are typically only taken down (1) after a candidate has accepted, (2) when the role has been reneged or cut, (3) because there was a strong internal candidate, or (4) when enough good external candidates are far enough down the interview pipeline that there's no need to collect more resumes. Your application mere days earlier may have been an exercise in futility. If you'd successfully developed a relationship and met with someone on the inside, they could either throw your resume in and stall the process so you could be seen, or tell you the position was filled already.

The other fear — that building relationships takes a lot of elbow grease that isn't guaranteed to pay off — is also valid. But think about it this way: if you're tailoring your resume appropriately before applying to jobs online, it takes at least an hour. Add another 45 minutes for updating your cover letter, too. It's a lot of effort before you even know if the role on paper matches the role in actuality, and whether sacrificing trivia night to send in your application was even worth it. If you spent the same two hours tracking down contacts at a company, you could potentially use the same amount of time to email every single person in the freaking department and cultivate several internal advocates for you. Yes, it takes work, but so does every other part of job hunting. Might as well make your time and effort work harder for you, right? If you're a proponent of working smarter, not harder, this tactic is a great place to start.

If you're trying to decide whether to spend your next 15 minutes meeting people or perusing job boards, here's your new guiding mantra: always seek the humans. Now that you know better, you'll get better results.

If you're making a drastic career change, you may not have a well-developed network in your target industry. That's okay — you just need to create one. The beginning of any network is connecting with one person, so ask yourself where people in your target company or industry would hang out. Would they be members of specific trade associations? Social media groups? Book clubs? Once you start brainstorming, you may realize you already know someone who works in the area who you can speak to. If not, you can even start with searching for people who work at your ideal company on LinkedIn, and send a heartfelt, genuine, and brief message asking to connect. For advice on ways to approach this and a script for a sample networking outreach message, visit GetCareerClarity.com/Bonus.

Once you form the first relationship, you can set up an informational conversation to learn about how they got into the industry and what steps they'd recommend someone take to transition into the sector. All you have to do in a conversation like this is have a few questions you're curious to ask about their unique experience. Bring up your query, and let them talk. Ask follow-up questions. Not every informational interview will be equally fruitful, but stay curious and listen for insights or connection points with the individual. Even if the conversation doesn't give you the answers you wanted, this first connection can point you in the direction of where to find others. And, if you ask for it, they might even be willing to warmly introduce you to other people they know who can help, too.

While the best time to plant your relationship trees was 20 years ago, the next best time is today. From watching hundreds of clients go through this process, I can assure you that most people are delighted to help you when you ask for something specific, but asking requires being vulnerable and courageous, the same skills we started developing in Phase 2. Vulnerability is a necessary condition for success.

When people start building connections in a new part of their network, folks get skittish about relationship development because they fear they have nothing of value to offer. It's a worry that no one will waste their time talking to you because you're a know-nothing nobody — and if you're part of an underrepresented group in the office, this fear can be amplified by having been written off or not taken seriously in the past.

If this fear is cropping up for you, remember that when you explored your Strengths pillar, you discovered all the ways your unique gifts have value in the world. However, it might be tricky to understand how to translate that value into one-on-one networking conversations. Here are a few new ways to think about these conversations when you feel like you're out of your league.

First, remember that the person said "yes" in the first place, so you don't need to prove anything. They've already agreed to talk with you, and you need to trust their judgment — they would have said "no" if they thought it would be a total waste of their time.

Second, when you ask someone to articulate why they love what they do, it helps them sharpen their thinking. Your innocuous questions might help them prepare for a future job opportunity, podcast interview, or even hone an impressive author biography for the back cover of their first book. You're giving them the gift of asking some of the both obvious and nuanced questions they haven't had to articulate aloud.

Third, when you're in an informational conversation, your goal is to learn about the problems and opportunities in the company, the team, and the role. You aren't meant to just passively consume that information. Do something with it: use the information to decide whether you're actually interested in a role there, see how it fits your 4 Pillars, and determine if you want to keep moving forward toward a possible formal interview. The point is to learn to ask insightful questions, listen deeply, and look for opportunities to serve and support the other person — critically important skills that will serve you in any job (and, for my aspiring entrepreneurs, translates beautifully to prospective sales conversations).

When you're listening, you can process the information you're hearing through the lens of "how might I be able to help solve that?" Heard someone mention that change management has been tough for their team, and you have a lot of experience smoothing over rough transitions? Offer that up. Share resources, give advice, or possibly even offer to come help in a part-time or full-time capacity.

This part often feels a lot scarier in concept than it does when you execute. Pick someone that you already know and ask if you can have a practice relationship-building conversation with them. Do a trial run of sharing about your transition and desired direction, and pepper them with questions about what they like about their job and where they see opportunities for growth at their company. If you dare, ask for their feedback or initial impression afterwards. This kind of loving, constructive feedback will help you feel more comfortable and confident in conversations like this with strangers.

Courageous outreach to people you don't know will be a critical part of your success: the data on effective networking consistently shows that "weak ties" — people on the outskirts of your friend circle who have different networks from yours — are best able to open new doors for you. Commit to going all-in, and start researching ways to expand your relationship ties.

Your first move after creating and refreshing your relationships and starting to build up a new brand is to complete some initial research into an organization or role that catches your eye, and ask yourself if this organization and opportunity align with your 4 Pillars. We've done this discernment and soul-searching to identify great-fit work for you in Phases 1 and 2, and it would be a shame for job search anxiety to cause you to throw it out the window and desperately snap up the first role you're offered, regardless of whether it aligns with your fulfillment drivers.

After you've done the initial research and gotten some data points that validate if the organization could be a great fit, your next step is to do further vetting through an informational chat with a leveraged, strategic relationship. This is where the relationship building you already started can come in handy. Either ask a contact to make an introduction for you if they can, or use your online sleuthing skills to find the email or phone number for someone at the company, and reach out to gather that important reconnaissance. Like we talked about in Chapter 16, the point of having an informational interview is for you to ask the bold, fearless questions and find out if the role, team, and organization fit you, so don't hold back. Playing small never serves you in the long run.

There are three likely outcomes from your informational conversation:

The gold medal outcome: The informational conversation goes brilliantly, you're totally sold on the organization, and your contact offers to open doors for you at the company so you don't even have to apply online. They might walk your resume straight to the hiring manager or HR screener or send an email introduction with you CCed and your resume attached. Nice work! You just bought a one-way ticket to a first round interview without even having to whisper "online applicant tracking system."

The silver medal outcome: The chat is helpful and validates that you want to pursue a role there, but the person can't make any additional internal introductions for you. Instead, use their insights to custom tailor your resume and cover letter to differentiate yourself from all the other online applicants. Make sure that all the test drives you've done in Phase 2 to vet this career path now show up as provable experience in some form on your resume, LinkedIn profile, and cover letter — including mentioning this person in your cover letter, to establish extra credibility with the HR team. Since your resume should function as a strategic marketing document, not the anthology of everything you've ever done, use the insights from your conversation to decide what to emphasize and what to omit. Remember Sam's story: if you don't cull down your professional story to only include your most impressive, relevant accomplishments, hiring managers might wonder if you know how to prioritize — or worse, assume you don't understand the value of your work.

The bronze medal outcome: You have the conversation and realize that, after you hear the "real deal" about the organization, you don't actually think the opportunity matches up with your 4 Pillars very well. So, you abandon ship, stop worrying about submitting an application there, and ask your contact if there are any similar companies/roles/sectors they'd recommend you take a look at. It might be disappointing, but it saves you tons of time and heartbreak in your job search — and nets you an introduction to someone else who might be able to help even more.

Taking the time to chat with someone on the inside is worth its weight in gold, even if you only snag a bronze medal outcome. If you don't do the informational interview, you're winging it on your application and could be wasting time sending applications to companies that violate the values you expressed in your 4 Pillars.

An alternate discovery you might make is that the company seems wonderful but isn't hiring right now, or doesn't have any roles posted online that quite fit you. This doesn't mean that you need to abandon all hope and head back to scouring online job boards again. You can use the strength of your new strategic relationships to pitch custom creating a job for you — just like you'd do if you haven't seen a particular job title that fits your unique skills.

Don't believe it's possible? Shanna is an example of someone who's had it happen. Shanna was a neuroscience PhD stuck working in academia and was itching to make a move into the private sector instead. For her first step out of the ivory tower, she'd successfully landed a new job at a research lab, but the culture was so toxic and abusive she felt both desperate to leave (again) and absolutely drained even thinking about job hunting one more time. When Shanna started creating an exciting vision for where she wanted her career to go, she got clear on the kind of employers she wanted to work for before she'd pinned down an exact job title. After creating her "short list" of target employers, Shanna set up an informational interview with a promising health tech company looking for more data points about the company's culture. Because she was clear on who she was and how she could help them, the hiring manager said the conversation had been so great that, even though they had just filled a role for someone exactly like her, they were going to the organization's board to custom-create a role for her that week. And they did.

Shanna's not alone. Earlier in her career, Nicole Iacovoni, MSW had a new role invented for her at a private therapy practice. And for Career Clarity certified coach Kate Solis Silva, almost every single opportunity she's had throughout her career has been custom tailored (or created from scratch) for her. I've had it happen myself:

an informational conversation with a prospective hiring manager started with her saying, "We're not hiring right now, but I'm happy to share information about our team." It ended 45 minutes later with her saying, "Sit tight and give us a few days to pull together an offer for you."

> "If it's meant to work, it's going to work. Flow, not force, and let things unfold.
>
> Kate Solis Silva

If you've done a handful of informational interviews, you might notice the most frustrating thing about them is that they don't always turn into an immediate job offer. That's okay. Having a company custom-create a role for you is thrilling but takes time. We call relationship development "seed planting" for a reason — these conversations need sufficient nurturing and time to germinate into the beautiful sprouts of possible job opportunities. That's why picking up a book like this before your hair's on fire and you rage-quit your job is immensely helpful: you buy yourself a bit more pressure-free time to plant the seeds.

Remember, in job hunting, priorities require patience.

If you're feeling antsy about the waiting game, lean on people in your support network. Tell them how anxious you are and how restless you're feeling. Ask them for ideas, encouragement, or funny cat memes to distract you and get you out of your head.

Shanna had no idea that her information-gathering conversations would result in a custom role for her. And she, Nicole, Kate, and I are all examples that if you trust the process and continually put yourself out there strategically, incredible opportunities can — and DO — present themselves. But if you don't take the initiative to ask, you may never find out what's possible.

Being assertive, pleasantly aggressive, and asking people to help you are three final steps to maximize the probability of your success in Phase 3.

If I had a dollar for every time someone asked me: "*Is it too soon to follow up?*" or "*Should I really bother them again?*" or "*Wouldn't that just make me annoying?*" I'd have enough money to close the gender pay gap across all races. Calling someone five times a day and emailing them just as often absolutely makes you annoying. But if you haven't sent at least two emails or phone calls/texts/social media messages to a contact of yours within a week, you're bordering on forgettable. People need to be reminded about how they can help you, and most people don't mind the nudges if they're polite and brief. I often tell coaching clients that if you aren't persistent, someone who isn't as smart, talented, or capable as you will start snapping up your opportunities because they're willing to be more assertive and follow up. Don't let that happen to you!

That's why Phase 3's tagline could be "go all out and go all in."

If you truly want a change, the best way to make it happen is to go above and beyond. Do the things that make you a little uncomfortable. Publish an analysis about your new industry on social media. Reach out to the person you haven't talked to in two years.

Fortune favors the bold, and taking consistent, courageous action puts you squarely in the middle of the road for when that good ol' luck truck trundles through.

A successful transition is available for you if you're willing to keep taking action to pursue it. Remind yourself what's on the other side: work you'll enjoy, problems that are meaningful to you, coworkers you genuinely like, and being paid what you need to create the life you want.

Don't let yourself spiral into overwhelm or give up. The career and life you've been dreaming of is just over that hill. Remember our baby steps: even tiny actions towards a stronger brand and network will start to pay dividends.

CLARITY QUESTIONS:

Where might be a few good places to start meeting people who work in the industries or companies you're curious about? (Brainstorm both offline and online.)

Who do you already know in those areas who might be willing to speak to you or introduce you to their contacts?

Who would be willing to do a test run informational interview conversation with you, to help you shake off any cobwebs and get some loving feedback?

CHAPTER 21

Why Your Journey May Include a False Summit

As you execute on the elements of Phase 3, you'll start to see traction in informational conversations, formal interviews, and job offers. This is exactly what you want — and it's a sign you've made it easy for people to see how great you are.

At this point, recovering perfectionists are tempted to put their feet up, take a load off, and complete their Career Clarity experience with a satisfied smile, reveling in never having to job search ever again.

And while we want to celebrate your accomplishments, how far you've come, and how much you've grown, there's one last thing you need to know about this career journey.

When you land that wonderful job offer and successfully make your career change, your Career Clarity journey might pause for now. However, you're not done with your career growth and evolution forever.

One thing that unites the kinds of people who embark on a career change journey is that they're always hungry to learn and grow. (I've taken to calling us, lovingly, "learning junkies.") The paradox of learning junkies is that we never stop wanting to be challenged. The craving to expand doesn't just go away when you get that great job. Learning junkies actually outgrow jobs faster than your average bear, and end up looking for new possibilities to keep expanding their knowledge.

When I first started leading people through career changes, this fact terrified me. I based the efficacy of my results on the permanence of the change. I was devastated when clients told me they'd made another shift. It took years to truly contextualize what was happening for my clients, and why it was actually a great thing they kept making moves.

After watching this growth and expansion cycle for several years, here's what I've seen: after moving through the Career Clarity process, you've discovered a direction that sparks joy and excitement in your bones. You've landed the job (or started the business), and are often flying high for months or years.

At some point, enough time has passed that some of the luster of the initially thrilling job wears off. Maybe some of the excitement dwindles as you settle in, or maybe a teammate's behavior starts to get on your nerves a little bit. There's an opportunity at this point to make minor adjustments to course-correct, perhaps by talking to your boss about the annoying coworker or starting a daily gratitude practice at the office.

But course-corrections don't always resolve everything, and as a growth-oriented person, you'll likely experience a shift in how the job "fits" you over time, no matter what. You might outgrow your work and master the job or perhaps realize that you don't want to stay on that team forever. You'll be evolving and changing as time goes on, and so will your values and needs. Almost inevitably, you'll find that your work doesn't match up quite as well with your values and needs anymore.

Sometimes it's because the work changes: they're asking you to work longer hours, violating your Lifestyle pillar, or your promotion ends up pushing you away from your strengths. Other times, it's because you're stagnating, feeling "bored out," or burned out. And yet other times, it's because you're fundamentally changing. Often, thrilling life changes can spur us to readjust our career paths: you got married, had your first baby, are expecting baby number three, got your master's degree, or moved to the city (or country) of your dreams.

Sometimes these fundamental changes are a product of disappointment or tragedy. Your divorce means you want your work hours to adapt to your custody schedule. The death of your loved one made you reevaluate what's most important to you right now and how you want to honor your values in your work. Maybe you've encountered a health problem that changes the way you work. I'm getting more familiar with this last one myself — while I've had scoliosis my entire life, it's suddenly become far more difficult to sit at a desk for hours on end. This health situation means either I resign myself to a life of constant pain medication so I "power through" work, or I choose to make adjustments to my lifestyle needs so my work matches my body's capabilities.

No matter the cause, there will come a moment when you realize your current role is no longer serving you. You'll feel a lot of feels: some days you're mad, some days you're heartbroken, some days you're afraid of changing anything. (If this sounds a heck of a lot like the Five Stages of Career Grief we talked about in Chapter 4, it's because it is.) You'll truly feel the depth and breadth of your feelings, and are presented with a Choose Your Own Adventure decision point: do I stay here, feeling the way I feel, or is it time for me to make a bigger shift? If you know someone who's constantly complaining about their job, is not fun to be around, and yet won't do anything to solve the problem, you know exactly what a Doldrum Debbie or Downer Dave looks like when they stay at a poor-fit job too long.

If you make the decision to do something about it, you move into a delightful and juicy introspective season where you reestablish who you are and what you want by doing lots of reflection, just like you did throughout this book. You'll probably want to reach for this book again when you hit this point in the future, and the running start you established in Phase 1 will help you reorient each time you face a new career question. In a lot of ways, you'll be seeing yourself with fresh eyes in a new season of life. It's time to envision what you want most and imagine a reprioritization of your life to better honor your current priorities and values. If it's truly transformational, it's probably going to get a little messy.

From here, you can grow right into your next career evolution, and can expect to be moving through this cycle over and over again throughout the rest of your career.

If you value learning, seeing this growth cycle might be a relief or even a joy! You can continue to follow your natural tendencies to expand and stretch your knowledge. It also means you're not broken or weird if you're outgrowing jobs. It's truly the natural order of things, and anything else would be fighting your humanness. Don't beat yourself up about the speed with which you notice yourself moving through this progression. There's natural variation with every learning junkie.

Back in Chapter 2, Jaime and Deja both thought they had their 4 Pillars prioritization and tradeoffs set up in a way that felt good. But after being in their jobs for a while, they each realized their truest priorities were different than what they'd initially thought. Those slight differences in tradeoffs and needs resulted in the desire to make another change.

Once Jaime understood her current pillars and priorities better, she accepted a job offer with another company that was in far better alignment with her pillars, and came with a $20K pay raise. And when Deja made the transition into her newest role, there weren't enough capital letters or exclamation points to contain her glee at finding the place that felt like it finally "fit" her.

Even if your circumstances change beyond your control, coming back to these tools can be helpful. Years after our work together, former teacher Julia from Chapter 1 sent me an update on how her career had been unfolding in the middle of the coronavirus pandemic and public health crisis that resulted in mass global unemployment and lucrative industries almost vanishing. She had loved what she'd been doing over the last three years, been promoted twice, and was on her way to leading a bigger team when the entire nonprofit folded overnight. Rather than beating herself up, feeling inadequate, or spinning in a directionless way, she came back to her 4 Pillars and quickly mobilized into action. In the span of 10 days, she found a different organization, landed an interview, got hired with a pay raise (in a recession, no less), and received the flexibility to work from home whenever she needed to. These tools will always be here when you need them, so you can bypass the valley of perpetual devastation and hike back into the meadow of soulful alignment.

No matter the reason for revisiting them, these tools will serve you. Over the years, I've spoken with alumni of the NFL, entrepreneurs, CEOs, Emmy award winners, and even a Victoria's Secret Angel who were all craving a change and learning something new. I've worked with people on every continent except Antarctica who were ready for a change. Desires for continual growth and expansion are natural, normal, and good for the soul.

I wish I could tell you there's a magical "silver bullet" formula for knowing exactly how to prioritize your pillars forever so you can check the boxes and kick up your feet until you retire. There's not one. But once you start taking steps in the direction you think fulfillment might lie, like Jaime, Deja, and the countless others you met in these pages, you'll notice what feels good and keep moving toward that. You'll also notice any fulfillment gaps quickly and learn the questions you need to ask so you can take impeccable care of your needs.

When you pair self-awareness with this framework, you'll have the skillset to powerfully and confidently make move after move throughout the years — and might actually have ice cream and puppies bursting forth from your computer before you know it.

Come back to this fulfillment framework anytime you need to audit your situation and figure out where you can make improvements, because you deserve work that helps you be your most alive, energized, joyful, fun self.

CHAPTER 22

Scaling the Summit of Mount Fulfillment

You've made it! You've learned the strategy — and the steps — to find a career that fits. You've scaled Mount Fulfillment and are taking your best sweaty, exhausted, accomplished selfie from the peak.

You might be treating yourself to some celebratory bubbly or delicious takeout to mark the night before you start your new job. You might be planning a vacation to somewhere tropical and sunny to celebrate the pay raise you just bagged. Or you might be reveling in knowing that you created more time to spend with friends and loved ones by ruthlessly defending your Lifestyle pillar.

No matter what flavor your success came in, it's a sweet victory.

While reaching the clarity summit of Mount Fulfillment is awesome, the process to finding a career that fits can be equally satisfying. You've discovered how to calibrate your inner GPS to lead you to your true north. You've learned the strategic framework to understand your fulfillment drivers and now know new ways to generate cool and creative career ideas. You know how to protect yourself by testing your ideas before making a move, and you know the most important factors to focus on when job searching.

These are tools and knowledge that you can use for the rest of your career — and your life.

Past client Lucia has come back to these tools over and over again in her awesome career path. When we first started working together, Lucia took the courageous step to leave a fundraising job in Los Angeles that looked great on paper but didn't fit her values. Through exploring the Career Clarity framework, she realized why such an impressive role didn't feel good for her: she was absolutely out of alignment on her Personality pillar, and wanted to prioritize finding an amazing group of people to work with. Her next move landed her at a prestigious media company in New York City, working for the most incredible team she'd ever met. That was a quantum leap of fulfillment and satisfaction improvement for her! But here's the kicker: after working at the media company for a while, she realized that her first courageous leap reminded her how capable and resilient she is, and she decided to take a second leap: starting her own location-independent business. She became a 30-something snowbird and started spending more time with her aging family members in Florida. Building up the courage and clarity to start her own business has had an incredible impact throughout her life, and has wonderful effects for her extended family, too.

Sounds pretty dreamy, doesn't it? Look at how some of these individuals you've met achieved their dreams, too:

- Deja is leading corporate social responsibility for a major media company while living and working abroad.
- Jaime is healthy and back to feeling properly balanced in her work and life.
- Ryan is becoming the kind of role model parent he wants his kids to have.
- Lucia is spending quality time with her aging parents.
- Annie is working from home so she can spend time with her 2-year-old daughter, with a five-figure pay bump.
- Lydia is spending more time with her partner and on hobbies that fill her soul up with joy.
- Aviva runs multiple profitable businesses and is there for her kids whenever they need her.
- Mohammed runs a mentorship program and is developing his leadership identity in the information technology sector.
- Ron got the six weeks of bonus paternity leave on top of a six-figure offer in a brand new city.
- Naomi is creating a new relationship with her family, and helping people in a totally different way in her new path.

- Maria is living out a dream of becoming an amazing doctor and a mom.
- Matt is back to feeling like himself again, reconnecting with his wife, and pursuing his interest in writing fiction.
- Shanna is in a custom-created job, developed just for her.

There's so much more available for your career and life. If you feel like you're in work that doesn't fit, trust that feeling. Act on that feeling. Explore what else is out there.

When Andi acted on that intuitive clarity, she transformed her life and her marriage. Andi and her husband were successful in their jobs in Ohio, but neither loved what they were doing. Her secret dream was to move closer to her family so they could cultivate a deeper relationship with them right now — not only as they were aging or had medical needs. Because Andi let herself articulate her deepest values and look for ways they could align with the work she truly wanted, she was able to land a fully remote consulting role with a raise and could work from her parents' home as often as she needed. Plus, her new flexible gig enabled her husband to start pursuing his dream of entrepreneurship, too.

People who follow this framework also report that it affects them in other, unexpected ways. Life as they know it changes forever because their trust in their own capabilities has fundamentally shifted. They start to reach for bigger challenges within their work. They increase their risk tolerance and contingency planning for trying career experiments. They give themselves permission to take creative sabbaticals or more incredible vacations. They feel less defeated by other people's opinions — and start surrounding themselves with more supportive, aspirational friends and mentors. They even start to upgrade other parts of their lives, like making different nutrition decisions because they value their body and brain differently.

This journey should change you. Defining success on your own terms and choosing a career that matters is a rebellious act.

> “ Let yourself have experiences that change you.
>
> My wonderful Aunt Beth

Life is short. You don't know if you have 60 days or 60 years left. Wouldn't you rather give yourself permission to be joyful, to pursue your dreams, and to lean into a little bit more career adventure?

As far as we know, we only get one shot at this precious, magnificent thing called life, so we might as well live it as if we don't get another one.

Remember that this career clarifying work is worth it. Your sense of meaning and purpose in your career is worth it. Your happiness is worth it.

You are worth it.

Additional Resources

Finding Help

If you've loved this book but don't want the party to stop just yet, there are tons more resources available for you online. At GetCareerClarity.com/Bonus, you can get all the complementary worksheets to go with each section of the book, register for a five-day Career Clarity challenge, take the Work Fulfillment Assessment to help you see which is your highest priority Pillar, take the assessments mentioned in the Personality section, hear full-length audio interviews with some of the individuals featured in the book, and discover ways to work with me and my team of certified Career Clarity coaches. You'll even find my list of Secret Weapon books and resources to keep you moving on your clarity journey. And if you're doing a Career Clarity book group, I've included a conversation guide to prompt further discussion and reflection for your group members. In short, there are tons of additional goodies I want to make sure you have so you're set up for success. Check them out at GetCareerClarity.com/Bonus today!

Personality Assessment Resources:

Myers-Briggs: www.16personalities.com
Enneagram: www.eclecticenergies.com/enneagram/test
Five Love Languages: www.5lovelanguages.com

If you applied any of these tools or used the resources from the book in your own life, let me know. You can reach me directly at Lisa@GetCareerClarity.com, and I'd love to send you a congratulations note and celebrate your successes with you.

Acknowledgements

> "If I have seen farther than others, it is by standing on the shoulders of giants.
>
> Isaac Newton

Thank you to the career experts who came before me, whose books I read, whose trainings I did, and who I got the honor of apprenticing under in my budding coaching career. Jenny Blake, Adrian Klaphaak, and Scott Barlow, I owe you one. A BIG one. Thank you for always believing in me, and pushing me to become better at my craft.

I owe an incredible debt of gratitude to the entire book launch team, and specifically the individuals who read an early version of the manuscript and offered their thoughtful, kind, insightful feedback. Thank you to Kelly, Todd, Kristie, Courtnee, Mike, Christina, Morgan, Brian, Nicki, Jenn, Kate, Donna, Maghan, and Chris – you made me and this book infinitely better, and it's because of you that this content turned out as helpful and actionable as it did.

To Tracie, my fabulous developmental editor, thank you for championing every personal anecdote, client story, and continuing to remind me that more commas aren't always better. Your support in growing into my voice as an author over the last three years has been invaluable. And to Brenna, for helping me maintain my sanity throughout the years. You've been an incredible right-hand woman to help Career Clarity serve and support so many people year after year.

And, of course, to Derek. Thank you for always seeing me through loving, supportive eyes, and for relentlessly pursuing my dreams with me. Thank you for your patience with reading rounds of book edits. I love you and am incredibly grateful to get to do life with you.

About The Author

If there's a job out there, Lisa Lewis Miller has probably done it. Lisa is a career change expert, author, and the founder of Career Clarity, a company helping individuals step into the careers they've been dreaming of.

Her path evolved into coaching after working in digital marketing for nearly a decade at companies like 2U, Edelman, the American Cancer Society, *Teen Vogue*, *Seventeen*, Network for Teaching Entrepreneurship, and CBS College Sports.

Lisa's work has been featured in *The Washington Post*, *Business Insider*, *US News and World Report*, *Fast Company*, *Forbes*, *Refinery29*, and more. She received her coaching certification as one of only seven coaches in the world trained in the Pivot Method. Clients praise her ability to see through their excuses, champion their possibilities, and give resume reviews that are like "purifying hellfire."

Lisa is from Colorado and received her bachelor's degree in economics from Barnard College in New York City.

If you're looking for someone who will believe in your potential career happiness as strongly as you do — and help equip you with the ideas and resources to make it happen — you can learn more about Lisa's work at GetCareerClarity.com.

Lightning Source UK Ltd.
Milton Keynes UK
UKHW012238060223
416577UK00010B/786/J